ROCK CLIMBING

A Guide to Skills, Techniques and Training

ROCK CLIMBING

A Guide to Skills, Techniques and Training

JACK GRIFFITHS

THE CROWOOD PRESS

First published in 2012 by
The Crowood Press Ltd
Ramsbury, Marlborough
Wiltshire SN8 2HR

www.crowood.com

© The Crowood Press 2012
Illustrations © The Crowood Press unless otherwise credited

All rights reserved. No part of this publication may be reproduced or transmitted in any form or by any means, electronic or mechanical, including photocopy, recording, or any information storage and retrieval system, without permission in writing from the publishers.

British Library Cataloguing-in-Publication Data
A catalogue record for this book is available from the British Library.

ISBN 978 1 84797 425 9

Dedication
To everyone I ever shared a rope with.

Acknowledgements
A big thank you to Steve Gorton (the photographer) and for photos donated, taken and posed for by Bea Griffiths, Lucy Johnson, Nolan Barnwell, Oli Lyon, James Grinstead, Brenden Harkness, Trystan Jones-Morris and Caroline Talbot. Many photos were taken at Camp 5 (the biggest and best climbing wall in South-East Asia) and at the Castle Climbing Centre in London. We also received support from Urban Rock, a fantastic climbing-specific shop and online retailer. Finally, a massive thank you goes to Bardy Griffiths (my mum) and to Caroline Talbot for her patience, proof-reading skills and support, I could not have done it without you.

Disclaimer
Please note that the author and the publisher of this book are not responsible or liable, in any manner whatsoever, for any damage, injury or adverse outcome of any kind that may result from practising, or applying, the techniques and methods and/or following the instructions described in this publication. Since the exercises and other physical activities described in this book may be too strenuous in nature for some readers to engage in safely, it is essential that a doctor is consulted before undertaking such exercises and activities.

Climbing, in all its forms, is an activity with inherent danger. Many of the hazards involved are unavoidable and nothing described in this book can remove the risks involved. It is very important that you read and accept the following participation statement set out by the British Mountaineering Council before participating in any climbing activity.

The British Mountaineering Council's Participation Statement:

'The BMC recognizes that climbing, hill walking and mountaineering are activities with a danger of personal injury or death. Participants in these activities should be aware of and accept these risks and be responsible for their own actions and involvement.'

Photos by Steve Gorton, except where indicated otherwise
Typeset by Jean Cussons Typesetting, Diss, Norfolk
Printed and bound in Singapore by Craft Print International Ltd

CONTENTS

Part 1: Introduction
1	Introduction to the Book	7
2	Climbing Styles	8
3	Grades	11
4	History	14
5	Ethics	15
6	Access	17

Part 2: Safety Skills
7	Bouldering	19
8	Top Roping	22
9	Sport Climbing	40
10	Trad Climbing	73
11	Multi-Pitch Climbing	107
12	Abseiling	118
13	Self-Rescue	133

Part 3: Climbing Technique and Training
14	Techniques	162
15	Technique Training	170
16	Mental Training	172
17	Physical Training	173
18	Final Thought	188

Index 189

CHAPTER 1

INTRODUCTION TO THE BOOK

This guide is designed to be a reference for those either just getting into the sport or experienced climbers who want to improve their rope work, technique and knowledge of rock climbing. My hope is that someone new to the sport will buy this book and grow with it, still finding it useful as a reference in years to come and to guide them forward with new skills as they develop as a climber.

Rock climbing is often misrepresented in the general press. Anyone who twists their ankle walking in Wales is greeted with the headline 'Climber Rescued Off Snowdon'. Climbing does cover a large variety of activities, each with a different set of rules, ethics and techniques. To me, someone who only climbs indoors is just as much a climber as someone who sport climbs, trad climbs, ice climbs or spends weeks on a Himalayan mountain.

This book will focus on indoor and summer rock-climbing. Along the way you will find a lot of jargon that you may or may not understand. I will do my best to make sure that these statements are explained in feature boxes at the bottom of each section. You should bear in mind, however, that climbing slang changes from region to region and country to country. An American 'hueco' is a British 'pocket' a French 'bloc' is a British boulder 'problem', so take all jargon with a pinch of local salt.

Before we get into the book, a word of warning: climbing at all levels has an inherent danger element to it. Using the right techniques, along with good route choice and experience, can all but eliminate these risks; however, there are some dangers completely out of your control. Rocks can, and do, just fall from cliffs, and being in the wrong place at the wrong time could be fatal. Nothing you will find in the pages of this book can completely remove the risks. The best way to avoid the hazards is to find a good instructor and learn from their experience. Ask at your local wall or search online for an instructor who can help you put the techniques and skills outlined in this book into practice.

I have been coaching and guiding for over ten years and have a massive respect for face-to-face practical teaching. I know from experience that a good coach can have a dramatic influence on your grade by improving your technique, strength, mental tactics and rope work. A weekend spent outside with an instructor can give you skills that would take years to learn from your friends, speeding up your progression and helping you to achieve your goals far quicker than you thought possible. This book should really be a backup to proper instruction, rather than a replacement for it; a reference before, or after, a lesson to remind you of the basic techniques involved.

OPPOSITE PAGE: *Trystan Jones-Morris stands in front of the Lotus Flower Tower, Canada.*
© JACK GRIFFITHS

CHAPTER 2

CLIMBING STYLES

This book will cover the following climbing styles.

Bouldering

Bouldering can be described as low-level climbing without ropes. It can be done in climbing walls, on boulders and at the base of crags, all over the world. It requires very little equipment and can be done alone or in a group.

Boulder problems can have a standing or sitting start, and can be from three to around six metres high. Anything higher starts to get a little scary and moves into the realm of soloing (climbing a route without ropes or protective equipment).

There are two types of protection for bouldering: boulder pads and spotters. The pad is a relatively hard piece of foam that is used to flatten out your landing and a spotter is someone at the bottom of your problem making sure you land on it.

Traversing (climbing sideways) at the base of cliffs or boulders is also popular, as you can climb for long distances without ever going more than a few feet from the ground.

Top Roping

This is generally done in climbing walls or as a way of practising routes outside. Top roping means that you are attached to a rope that goes to the top of the route. The other end of the rope is held by your partner, who uses a belay device to ensure that they can hold you should you fall off. This gives you the maximum degree of safety while climbing. So long as your partner holds the rope correctly, any fall should result in you comfortably hanging in your harness. Pretty much all climbing walls have these ropes in place, and top roping is the standard starting point for most climbers.

It should be noted that a few crags can only be climbed in this way. Southern Sandstone, for instance, in South-East England has rocks that are extremely soft in nature. If you used any other type of protection the rock would crumble away, putting the climber in danger and damaging the rock. The local guidebook will give you the best information about the ethics for your chosen venue.

Sport Climbing

In sport climbing (or lead climbing) the rope is not pre-placed at the top of your chosen route. There will be, however, a line of bolts up the route with a lower-off at the top.

The idea is that you stand at the bottom of a route with your partner, with the rope neatly laid out on the floor. As the climber, you tie into one end of the rope and your partner holds on to it using a belay device, giving you just enough slack to climb freely up the wall. You clip a quickdraw (see next chapter) to the bolts and the rope to the other side of the quickdraw, and then continue up the wall. If you fall off above one of the bolts, then you will fall approximately double the distance from your position to the last bolt. So long as your partner does not give out too much slack, there should be

John Chapel bouldering in Fontainbleau.
© STEVE GORTON

Caroline Talbot top roping at the Castle Climbing Centre, London.

little chance of falling to the floor. The lower-off marks the end of your climb. Lower-offs generally consist of two bolts linked together with a chain; this is threaded (discussed later) so that you can be lowered back to the ground.

Traditional (Trad) Climbing

Trad and sport climbing are similar except that there are no bolts or lower-offs when trad climbing. Instead, trad climbers use a variety of equipment to protect themselves while they are climbing and to attach themselves to the rock.

You start the same way you would when sport climbing but with some extra equipment on your harness (see next chapter). As you climb up the wall, you will stop every three metres or so and place a piece of gear into the rock, which you treat the same as you would a bolt in sport climbing. I should point out that you may not be able to place gear at such regular intervals. You may place four pieces of protection before tackling a difficult section of the route, or indeed be forced to climb for longer than intended before you find a place to put some worthwhile gear.

As there are no lower-offs on trad routes, you generally finish at the top of the crag. At this point you attach yourself to something solid (a tree, large boulders or multiple pieces of protection) and bring your partner up the climb on top-rope. Your partner will remove the gear from the route on their way up, leaving the route as you found it. You will then either walk or abseil back down.

Some crags have a mixed ethic where there will be a few bolts in places and so there is no possibility of placing your own gear. Some routes will have belay stations in place, even though the climbing is protected traditionally; this style is found in some places in the Alps and in the US.

Trad climbing requires more judgment and more skills than sport climbing but the reward is an amazing feeling of achievement and self-reliance. Trad routes tend to follow natural lines up your chosen cliff, which makes for great quality and memorable climbing. It is often said that trad climbing is dangerous but this is rarely said by those who practice it, and almost always by those who have never tried it. If you choose your routes carefully and get some good instruction on how to place good gear, and all the other skills discussed later in this book, then there is no need for it to be any more or less dangerous than sport climbing or bouldering.

Multi-Pitch Routes

If your rope is sixty metres long, then this is the maximum distance you can climb from your partner. However, many cliffs you may wish to climb are longer than sixty metres, so how do you get to the top?

The technique is to break the route down into sections or pitches. If your route is ninety metres long, you might climb up thirty metres, anchor yourself to the wall and bring your partner up to join you. Your partner may now climb the

Ben Watts places a wire above the sea on Baggy Point, North Devon. © JAMES GRIMSTEAD

Alek Scorupa sport climbing in the Gorge du Loupe. © STEVE GORTON

Pete Smith and Kat Freeman just past half way on the Chief, Squarmish, Canada. © JACK GRIFFITHS

10 CLIMBING STYLES

The author soloing Heaven Crack, Stanage, the Peak District. © STEVE GORTON

next thirty metres and anchor themselves in and bring you up to join them. If you repeat this process, you can climb a cliff of any height. So long as you have food, water, light and good weather you can continue indefinitely, pitch after pitch after pitch.

This book will also look at abseiling and self-rescue. Although these are not climbing styles as such, they are invaluable skills that require a little practice but could be the difference between getting back to your bed or spending the night shivering in the rain, wishing you had read the chapter on self-rescue.

The styles listed below are not covered by this book but are described for completeness.

Soloing Climbing routes without protective equipment. All you will need are climbing shoes, chalk and a very strong mental ability to keep calm. To be taken very seriously.

Deep Water Soloing (DWS) This is the same as soloing but generally done with a large body of water underneath you at all times. Falls from under ten metres are generally safe but a ten-metre belly flop will sting somewhat. Falls from above ten metres can become very dangerous. DWS uses a grading system S0 to S3. S0 will be pretty much as safe as it gets. S3 is more like shallow puddle soloing and must be taken as seriously as soloing.

Aid Climbing All the climbing described later in this book is free-climbing, which means you use the equipment only to protect you should you fall off. Aid climbing uses the equipment specifically to gain height up your chosen route. It is graded from A0 to A5. A0 is generally a small section of your route that you cannot free climb, so you resort to pulling on the equipment. A5 requires great skill and nerve. You will encounter long sections of extremely poor (body weight only) protection.

Winter Climbing Winter climbing can be described as any climbing that requires the use of ice axes and crampons. There are many different styles from pure ice-climbing to Himalayan mountaineering. The objective dangers involved are significant and varied, going out into the hills in winter conditions without the relevant equipment and knowledge could get you into a lot of trouble.

Oli Lyon ice climbing.

Simon Thompson on a classic S0 DWS in Portland, UK. © JACK GRIFFITHS

> **JARGON**
>
> **Belay device:** a device used to control the rope of a climber.
> **Boulder problem:** a short route, up to twelve moves long, that does not require ropes for protection.
> **Crampons:** spiky plates attached to the soles of rigid boots to give purchase on ice and snow.
> **Ice axe:** a small, hand held, pick axe shaped tool used to climb ice and snow.
> **Lower-off:** the point marking the end of a sport route, usually consisting of two bolts linked by a chain.
> **Placing gear:** equipment placed into cracks that can then be used to attach the climber to the rock.

CHAPTER 3

GRADES

Climbing has many different disciplines, and the differences between them can be massive. It is pretty obvious that scaling Mont Blanc is as far away from bouldering as riding a bike is to Formula 1. It would be impossible to have a grading system that could tell you the difficulty of a four-metre boulder problem that could also tell you the details of an alpine ridge. So over the years each climbing style has developed its own grading system that can give you a good idea of what you are about to get yourself into.

So why do we grade our routes? Well there are a few reasons.

First, when you are flicking through a guidebook looking for the best crag to go to the following day, you can make sure that when you turn up there will be a selection of routes that you can warm up on and a selection of routes that you can push yourself on afterwards. If you were going sport climbing, most accomplished climbers would be looking for a few routes in the 5s, 6s and 7s to make sure they can have a good day at that venue. However, a beginner might be looking for routes in the 3s, 4s and 5s and would find the first venue extremely frustrating.

Second, there is the safety side. Matching up your ability to the route you are about to do can ensure that you don't climb yourself into trouble. This is especially true of traditional climbing where you can easily find yourself climbing into more and more serious positions.

Finally, there is ego. This is not to say that this is a bad thing. We often define ourselves by our abilities, and climbing can be at its most rewarding when we are improving. Unless you are the best climber in the world, you will always look at someone else and say 'If only I could climb as well as them, then I would be happy' and this is a good motivator to get you training. Grades can also be very useful as benchmarks and for goal-setting. You might say to yourself at the beginning of the season that you want to climb three 6bs by the end of the year, or a particular route at your local crag. This gives you constant reason not to let go when your arms are screaming with lactic acid in your training session, or make you spend a few extra seconds after every boulder problem wondering 'How could I do that a little more efficiently', rather than heading straight to the pub to celebrate.

So, as discussed above, there are different grades for different styles, but unfortunately there are also different grades in different countries. The charts below will match them up.

Bouldering

There are two bouldering grading systems in popular use. The American system or V grades and the French system developed in Fontainebleau or Font grades.

The trouble with the Font grades is that they sound almost exactly the same as French sport grades but they do not relate to each other at all. I would not expect a Font 6a move on a French 6a sport route, so for clarity I prefer the V grading system. You may have noticed that there is only one + in the V grades, that of V8+; this has been a relatively recent addition, basically to match up the Font and V grades. The limitation of the V grading system is that you can be quite a good climber but still only be climbing V3, which is much more impressive than it sounds.

When talking about bouldering grades, I tend to use the V grading system so that

BOULDERING GRADES

USA V grades	French Font Grades
V0–	Font 3
V0	Font 4
V0+	Font 4+
V1	Font 5
V2	Font 5+
V3	Font 6a / 6a+
V4	Font 6b / 6b+
V5	Font 6c / 6c+
V6	Font 7a
V7	Font 7a+
V8	Font 7b
V8+	Font 7b+
V9	Font 7c
V10	Font 7c+
V11	Font 8a
V12	Font 8a+
V13	Font 8b
V14	Font 8b+
V15	Font 8c

no one gets confused and thinks I'm talking about sport climbing.

Route Climbing

The main route-climbing grades, in regular use, are the UK, French, US and Australian systems. There is also a UIAA system and an Alpine system that are useful if you are getting into Alpinism, but to keep it simple I have left these out. If you are going somewhere that uses these grades, there will normally be a chart at the front of the guidebook that you can use to match up the grading system you know to the one in use in that area. For the majority of climbers the

12 GRADES

ROUTE GRADES

UK Technical Grade	French Sport Grade	USA Trad and Sport	Australian Trad and Sport
	1	5.1	4
	2	5.2	6
	2+	5.3	8
	3-	5.4	9
	3	5.5	10
3c	3+	5.6	12
4a	4	5.7	14
4b	4+	5.8	16
4c	5	5.9	17
5a	5+	5.10a	18
5b	6a	5.10b	19
	6a+	5.10c	19/20
	6b	5.10d	20
5c	6b+	5.11a	21
	6c	5.11b	22
	6c+	5.11c	23
6a	7a	5.11d	23/24
	7a+	5.12a	24
6b	7b	5.12b	25
	7b+	5.12c	26
6c	7c	5.12d	27
	7c+	5.13a	28
	8a	5.13b	29
7a	8a+	5.13c	30
	8b	5.13d	31
7b	8b+	5.14a	32
	8c	5.14b	33
	8c+	5.14c	34
	9a	5.14d	35
	9a+	5.15a	36
	9b	5.15b	37

aforementioned systems are more than enough.

The British technical grade is only ever used with its adjective grade (this will be discussed in detail below), and only loosely matches up with the other systems. The French grading system is only used for sport climbing and is not normally used when traditional protection is required. The American and Australian systems make no indication as to whether the route is bolted or traditionally protected; this information will be found in the local guidebook.

For clarity I will use the French grades when talking about sport climbing for the duration of this book.

British Traditional Climbing

Trad climbing in the UK has two systems that marry together to give some good information about a route before you have even read the description. The adjective grade came from when climbing was in its infancy in Britain and someone in stiff leather boots with a hemp rope around their waist did a route and claimed it to be 'Difficult'. Then they did another route that was a bit harder and claimed it to be 'Very Difficult' (and I'm sure it was, you wouldn't catch me climbing in my walking boots with nothing more than a stiff upper lip for protection!). Eventually the grade got to

GRADES

Extremely Severe (or XS) and from there they broke it down into E1, E2, E3, and so on.

But what you really need to know before heading up a traditionally protected route is how much protection you can expect to find. Will you be forced to leave your last piece of gear a long way behind while you head into territory that will test your physical capability or will you have a perfect wire placement just below the short difficult section (often referred to as the 'crux')? This is where the British trad grading system comes into its own. If you know that a reasonably protected E1 will be 5b, then any E1 5b you choose should be acceptably protected for the technical difficulty of the route. However, if you head up an E1 5a then you know that it will require bold climbing but at a lower technical grade. Conversely, an E1 5c will generally have a short, difficult 'crux' that will be very well-protected. So if your technical limit was 5a, you would have to be a very bold individual to take on an E1 5a, but a VS 5a would be hard but safe by comparison.

Using this system then, so long as you know what the average technical grade is for the adjective grade, you can know how bold your chosen route will turn out.

> **JARGON**
>
> **Adjective grade:** the word part of the British traditional grades.
> **Crag:** rocky outcrop.
> **Crux:** the hardest part of your route, problem or pitch.
> **Mont Blanc:** highest mountain in Europe.
> **Wire placement:** traditional protection.

BRITISH TRADITIONAL GRADES

UK Adjective Grade	Poor Protection	Average Protection	Well Protected
Moderate			
Difficult			
Very Difficult			
Hard Very Difficult			
Severe			4a
Hard Severe	3c	4a	4b
Very Severe	4a	4b	4c / 5a
Hard Very Severe	4b/4c	5a	5b
E1	5a	5b	5c
E2	5a	5b/5c	6a
E3	5b	5c	6a
E4	5c	6a	6b
E5	6a	6a/6b	6b
E6	6a	6b	6c
E7	6b	6c	7a
E8	6b	6c	7a
E9	6c	7a	7b
E10	7a	7a/7b	7b

CHAPTER 4
HISTORY

There is evidence of people climbing for well over 1,000 years. This activity, however, was generally for some other purpose rather than just for the pure pleasure or challenge that the piece of rock in front of them held. People climbed to find food such as bird's eggs, to shelter in caves or search for rare gems. It's only since the later 1800s that we have had a history of routes being climbed purely for their technical merit and that climbing has become a pastime in its own right.

Although there was much activity before it, W. P. Haskett Smith's solo ascent of Napes Needle in the Lake District in 1886, was so well publicized that it became known as the start of British rock climbing and inspired a generation of rock climbers to get out and create the sport as we know it today. Within the same decade, many ascents where being made all over Europe and the USA, which sparked the start of the sport in earnest.

Up to the time of the Second World War rock climbing and mountaineering expanded rapidly with many British ascents of routes up to E1 and some of the harder Alpine faces being ascended, such as the North Face of the Eiger in 1938. This progress was held up by the war but when it ended, a surplus of affordable pitons, carabiners and ropes were suddenly available and climbing started again with vigour.

Although there is record of bouldering being used as training for mountaineering in Fontainebleau near Paris, the father of modern bouldering is generally thought of as John Gill, who was quietly training and bouldering in America in the 1950s. Before Gill, who had a gymnastics background, no one had used chalk or trained specifically for climbing. He put up the world's first V8 in 1957 and the first V9 in 1959. This is an incredible achievement, considering that many modern climbers with the most technical shoes and training facilities can only dream of these grades over fifty years later. The top boulderers of our generation are climbing problems graded V15, but they all owe a debt to this pioneer of the sport.

The US in the 1950s was an exciting place to be for a rock climber, and the first ascent of the Nose on El Capitan in Yosemite was a pinnacle point for many in that decade. The route was climbed almost completely using aid (using equipment to gain height rather than to protect a fall) and took forty-five days to complete.

The next twenty years or so saw grades pushed and equipment improve, and many significant ascents. However, in 1980, when Boreal started to produce climbing shoes with the sticky rubber we know today, everything changed. A few climbers took advantage of this, along with dedicated training routines, to push the limits of sport climbing pretty much to where they stand today. Jerry Moffatt's ascent of Liquid Amber (8c/+), Ben Moon's Agincourt (8c) and Hubble (8c+), along with Wolfgang Gullich's Action Direct (9a), all in the early 1990s, set the standard for the next generation. Even now, twenty years on, only a handful of climbers climb at these grades. 9a+ is pretty much the top grade, with a couple of the best in the world claiming new routes at 9b, but no route at this grade has currently been repeated and therefore confirmed.

Traditional climbing has developed pretty much in tandem with the advent of better equipment, along with the same training mentality that goes with sport climbing and bouldering. Originally, climbers used hemp ropes and techniques that would be unheard of in today's trad climbing world. For instance, some early climbers would fill their pockets with an array of pebbles, which they would wedge into cracks, and then thread for protection. These days we carry nylon ropes that can absorb massive loads, wires that place quickly, cams that can make use of parallel cracks, slings and quickdraws that are lightweight, not to mention chalk and climbing shoes. Trad has reached its current height of E11 7a with Dave MacLeod's ascent of Rhapsody, and many modern climbers are climbing at levels that only the elite would have thought possible back in the middle of the last century.

So what for the future? Well, maybe the next generation will benefit from some sort of anti-gravity protein shake and will be warming up on 9a, but I personally think that routes will increasingly become more and more specialized, and in this way harder routes will go up but will see very few repeats.

There are, however, still climbing achievements to be had. El Capitan was originally climbed in 1958 in forty-five days with exclusive use of aid. In 2005, Tommy Caldwell climbed two routes on El Cap in 24h, free climbing both of them (only using his hands and feet to gain height), a monumental effort. In 2010, Leo Holding and James Pickles put up a new free route on El Cap, which just goes to show that there are still new routes to be had and old routes to be done in better style.

> **JARGON**
>
> **A free route:** a route that has been climbed with no use of aid climbing techniques.
> **Free climbing:** only using your body to gain height.
> **Pitons:** blades of metal used as protection for climbing; they are hammered into seams or cracks.

CHAPTER 5

ETHICS

The ethical debate is as much a part of climbing now as it was in the infancy of the sport. Each country has come up with different rules regarding how to treat the rock; this needs to be recognized by anyone heading away from their local crags. Below are a few issues you may come across.

Pitons Pitons (or pegs) are blades of metal that are literally hammered into the rock for use as protection; they are like a bolt that can be placed relatively easily on lead. The trouble with pitons is two-fold: they damage the rock and they degrade over time so that a route that may have been safe on the first ascent, can be very dangerous a few years later. Pitons are widely used in the Alps but are almost completely shunned in the UK. A famous incident occurred in 1936 when two climbers from Germany put up a route on Tryfan in North Wales (Munich Climb). They used two pitons in their ascent, which caused outrage amongst the local climbers who promptly made a second ascent without the use of their pitons, which were then removed.

Bolts Nowadays the debate surrounds bolts rather than pitons. In continental Europe, bolting is commonplace, as there is a seemingly endless amount of rock to climb, much of which is limestone that does not lend itself well to traditional protection. In the UK, however, there are far fewer climbing areas, and the rock is well-suited to traditional protection. This means that, generally, bolting is only allowed in established sport-climbing areas, which tend to be disused quarries, and in certain areas, such as Portland on the south coast, where there are almost no solid cracks to place protection. In some places in America and Europe they have a mixed ethic, where a bolt will be placed (generally by the first ascentionist)

A range of brand new, un-used pitons.

A rusty peg placed in a sea cliff. This peg was once a strong and reliable piece of protection, it is now extremely questionable.
© STEVE GORTON

ETHICS

This bolt has been glued into the rock. © STEVE GORTON

This bolt is an expansion bolt with a hanger. © STEVE GORTON

that will protect a section of the route that is otherwise unprotectable or create an easy aid section to bridge a gap in an otherwise free route. Some long routes will have bolted belays but are otherwise traditionally protected.

Chipping and Gluing In some places in Europe it is deemed fine to glue a hold back onto the wall if it comes off, or even chip or drill a hold into the wall if the person putting up the route feels a section is too hard. In the UK, and most of the US, either of these actions could cause outrage on a wide scale.

Rock Routes with Ice Axes As winter climbing has pushed its levels, there has started to be a trend of people climbing rock routes in mild winter conditions (just a bit of snow rather than a solid layer of ice). Climbing classic or popular routes with ice axes and crampons damages the rock and is not acceptable.

Gardening Many routes have been cleared of vines and foliage in the search for new lines. However, many endangered plants and wildlife rely on these environments, so we could be unknowingly killing off an endangered species in search for a new climb. It may be illegal in some places too, so be careful before taking your secateurs to the crag.

Drying Holds I know what it is like when you head to the crag to find the first hold of your project is sopping wet. In the past, some people used a blowtorch to dry the holds but I'm afraid this has been shown to weaken the rock significantly and is no longer acceptable. A towel and a windy day is the only answer.

Chalk or Pof? Chalk is almost universally used these days. However, in some places, Fontainebleau for instance, it is frowned upon. They prefer to use Pof, which is a resin that is kept in a small, porous bag that is slapped onto your hold, making a 'pof' sound. The resin left behind makes the holds stickier and leaves no white marks. However, it polishes up the hold vastly quicker than chalk, leaving many classic problems almost unclimbable, as all the friction has been lost from over-pofing. For that reason, it is absolutely NOT allowed in the UK.

ETHICS: IN SHORT

- Do not damage the rock or environment in any way.
- Respect local ethics, even if they are different to your own.

CHAPTER 6

ACCESS

In a perfect world, all climbing would be located on public land and managed by the local climbing club or national council. However, many crags are located on private land and access has been carefully negotiated. Landowners have much to worry about when people tramp across their land to go climbing on their cliff. Not least the chance of being sued. If people do have an accident, they need to remember that it was they who chose to go there and do that activity, and suing over your twisted ankle could have the knock-on effect of stopping much of the access to many crags across the world, as landowners get wind of such incidents. In the past, climbers have created other problems with access by leaving rubbish and faeces at the crag, making lots of noise, arguing with landowners and breaking property, such as fences or gates.

Crags may also be subject to seasonal restrictions due to nesting birds or other wildlife considerations. It is very important to respect these conditions or we may find that the whole area is closed to us, even though the birds are only there for a few months of the year. Climbing a route covered in bird poo, whilst being dive-bombed by a group of angry gannets, is no fun anyway!

You can normally find access information in the guidebook, on websites or sometimes on posters at your chosen crag's normal car park.

ACCESS: IN SHORT

- Make sure you have the right to go to your chosen crag.
- Treat landowners and the environment with respect.

JARGON

First ascentionist: the first person to climb the route.
Gannets: large, aggressive seabirds that nest on cliffs.
Lines: another word for routes.

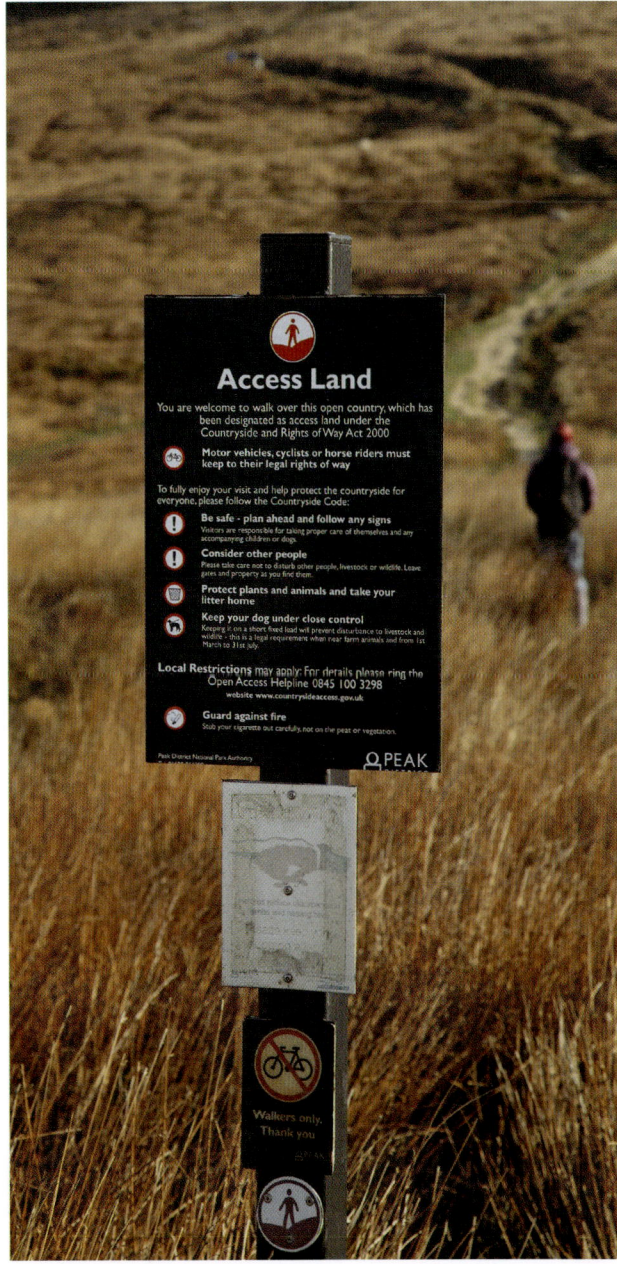

An entrance to the Peak District National Park.
© STEVE GORTON

PART 2
SAFETY SKILLS

CHAPTER 7

BOULDERING

Bouldering Kit List

Climbing Shoes

Climbing shoes are like ballet shoes with a rubber sole. They need to have a snug fit as, if they are loose, then they will not have the required rigidity when standing on small edges. A good way to get an idea for the shoe you need to buy is as follows: sit on a chair with your bare feet flat on the ground, now comfortably scrunch up your toes, the shoe that would be perfect for you would fit exactly around this shape of your foot. There are many different manufacturers, each with slightly different shapes and it is best to try on several different styles while talking to an experienced shop assistant. People often wear shoes that are so tight that they are in pain, but this is not recommended. How are you going to concentrate on climbing to your limit if your feet are in agony?

Chalk and Chalk Bag

Chalk is widely used to dry the sweat off your hands before or during a climb. It is frowned upon in some climbing areas, as it leaves white marks on the rock. Its use, however, has become almost universal and most climbers could not imagine climbing without it. Chalk comes either loose, as a block or in a mesh ball. Chalk balls reduce the amount of chalk that is spilt onto the floor or permeates into the

Tom Reeves being spotted by Anthony Carney at the Plantation, Stanage in the Peak District. © STEVE GORTON

BOTTOM RIGHT: *Lace-up, slip-on and Velcro climbing shoes.*

OPPOSITE PAGE: *Traditional gear.* © STEVE GORTON

20 BOULDERING

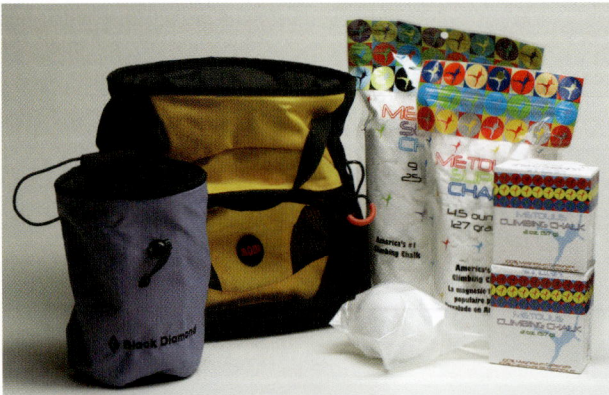

A selection of chalk bags and chalk.

A boulder pad folded up ready to be carried to the crag.

Trystan Jones-Morris being spotted while bouldering in the Peak District.

air and so is the preferred option for indoor climbing walls. There is little technical about the bag. You can buy bouldering-specific chalk bags that are like large, soft buckets of chalk, but most people carry a small bag tied around their waist.

Boulder Pad

When bouldering indoors, there is usually flat matting underneath the wall to soften your landing. Outdoor boulderers take a boulder pad with them, which is a square of hard foam that can be carried on your back. This is then placed at the bottom of the problem; you are trying to make the landing flatter and slightly softer, so that you don't bruise you heels on the rocks below.

Spotters

A couple of friends at the bottom are often used to make sure the pad is positioned in the right place and to help you land correctly should you fall off unexpectedly.

How It All Works

You and a couple of friends pack up your shoes, chalk, pads and other essentials for the day (food, tea, etc.) and head to your bouldering venue. On arrival, you find a problem you want to do. The pads are laid out at the base of the problem and you each take turns trying to get to the top. If you are climbing, then your friends stand at the bottom spotting. When you get to the top or fall off, your friends have a go and you take your turn as a spotter. Once you have all had enough of that particular problem, you move on. Repeat until it is time to head home.

Bouldering Safety Skills

The safety skills required for bouldering are minimal, but the hazards are great. The trouble with bouldering is that when you fall off, you fall to the floor. In a perfect world, you would only ever fall off in control. Generally, you will know when you are about to fall and you will be able to make a few slight adjustments to be sure of landing on your feet. Sometimes, however, a foot or hand may slip unexpectedly, or a hold could break off and that is when having a good spotter and a well-placed boulder pad makes all the difference.

Boulder Pads

When using boulder pads outside, try to make sure that the landing zone is as flat as possible. An uneven landing site can easily twist an ankle or worse. A rocky landing zone can sometimes be evened out by placing rucksacks or coats underneath the pad.

Make sure you look at the pads' placement in relation to the problem you are about to do. Many routes will veer off to the left or right, which may mean that you arrive at the last moves with your pads way off to the side and now useless. As a spotter, you must keep the pads in the best position throughout the climber's attempt of the problem.

Boulder mats indoors or outside are by no means a safety net. The majority of accidents in climbing walls occur in the bouldering area. Twisted ankles and worse limb injuries are common indoors and out. A good respect for this danger, and climbing with experienced boulderers, will not only reduce this risk but also create an encouraging atmosphere to help you climb better.

> **BOULDER PADS: IN SHORT**
>
> - The flatter your landing area, the better.
> - Your boulder pad is not a complete safety net.

> **SPOTTING: IN SHORT**
>
> - Keep a clear, flat landing zone.
> - Help your climber to land on their feet.
> - Be encouraging.
> - Give your climber your complete attention.

Spotting

First, a spotter makes sure that the climber has a clear landing area and ensures that the pad is placed in the best position. They make sure other people do not walk underneath the climber and that no one has left an ankle-twisting water bottle or other hazard in the landing zone.

Second, they will help the climber to land correctly. Depending on the situation, this could mean just placing their hands on the climber's back when they land to make sure they have their balance, or it might be a little more physical. If the boulder problem puts the climber in an awkward position with their back to the floor, then a good spotter may be able to support them during a fall, even changing their direction, and land them softly on their feet. This takes timing and strength, and cannot be learnt from this book – experience is the only way to improve.

The third responsibility is to be encouraging. There is nothing like your friends shouting at you to help you pull that little bit harder.

Finally, it is important to realize that spotting is a real responsibility. The difference between good spotting and bad spotting is massive, but the main thing you want from your spotter is their complete attention. Watching your friend struggle over a bulging top out while you drink tea is not spotting!

> **JARGON**
>
> **Problem:** a route up the boulder or bouldering wall.
> **Top out:** the final moves of a problem or route that finishes stood on top of the boulder (or wall).

Nick Durrand paying full attention while spotting Eleanor Moore in Fontainbleau, France.
© STEVE GORTON

CHAPTER 8

TOP ROPING

Top Roping Kit List

Shoes

See Chapter 7 for climbing shoe details.

Chalk and Chalk Bag

See Chapter 7 for details of chalk and chalk bags

Harness

Most people will wear a sit harness. If you are pregnant, overweight or very young (five years or below), you may need a full body harness. A sit harness requires your waist to be smaller than your hips, so that you cannot slip out of it. A big difference between harnesses is the buckles that they use. Some have a single metal buckle that is used to tighten and lock off the waist belt (I will call this the double-back system). Others have two metal buckles (one on top of the other) that keep the waist belt locked, and just need to be tightened (I will call this the zip-lock system).

Most harnesses have two tie-in points: one on the waist belt and one on the leg loops; these are connected by a belay loop. The tie-in loops have wear

LEFT: Caroline Talbot top roping in the Castle Climbing Centre, London.

A harness with doubled-back buckles.

A doubled-back buckle.

TOP ROPING

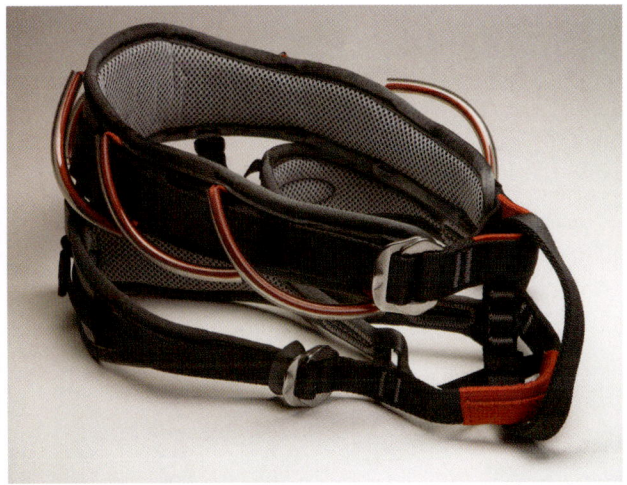

A harness with zip-lock buckles.

A zip-lock buckle.

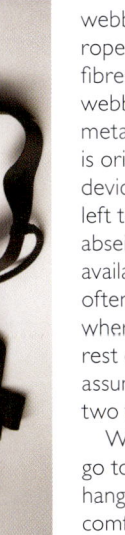

A full body harness.

> **BUYING A HARNESS**
> - Make sure it is the right size.
> - Make sure it suits the style of climbing you want to do.
> - Try on many styles with the help of an experienced shop assistant.

webbing around them, so as to stop the rope rubbing into the load-bearing fibres. The belay loop has no wear webbing, as it only ever has smooth metal rubbing against it. Your belay loop is orientated in such a way that the belay device sits top to bottom rather than left to right, which makes belaying and abseiling smoother. Hire harnesses, available from your local climbing wall, often have a single tie-in/belay loop, where everything is attached. For the rest of this chapter (and book) I will assume you have bought a harness with two tie-in loops.

When buying a harness it is good to go to a shop that has somewhere to hang from to make sure it is comfortable when in use. Make sure the harness fits properly; people often buy harnesses that are too small or too big. Think carefully about what you are going to be doing in your harness. If you are going to be multi-pitch trad climbing, you want something with at least four gear loops and a big comfortable waist belt. If you are only ever going to sport climb, then a lightweight, simple harness with two gear loops may be perfect. The answer is to get the help of a good shop assistant or do a lot of research before parting with your cash.

Belay Device

There are many devices on the market at the moment. The main differences between them are the amount of friction they generate, the thickness of rope they can work with and whether they have assisted braking or not. We will look closely at how to use these devices later, but for now be aware of these two popular types of devices: tubular belay devices, such as the Black Diamond ATC, and assisted-braking devices, such as the Petzl GRIGRI.

Tubular devices require the user to lock the dead rope away from the climber in order to arrest a fall. The device creates friction by forcing the rope to take two

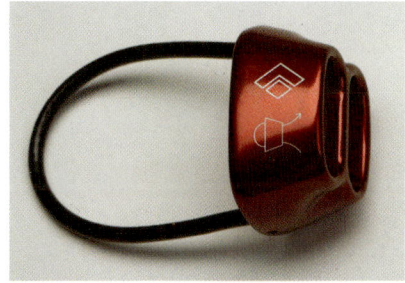

A standard tubular belay device (Black Diamond, ATC).

TOP ROPING

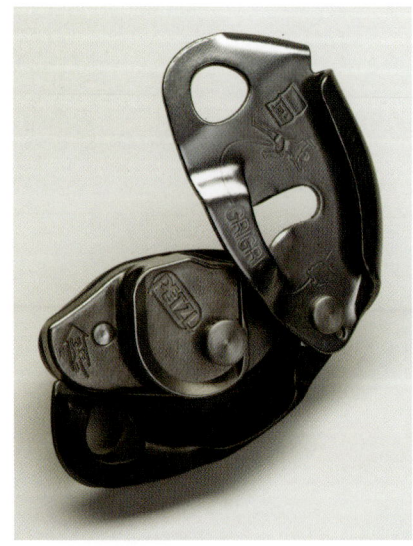

A Petzl GRIGRI 2.

180-degree turns in a short space (the smaller the space, the more friction the device creates). They are extremely versatile, they are relatively simple to use and can be used for both belaying and abseiling. Most are equipped with two holes and can therefore be used for double ropes and retrievable abseils; both of these skills will be looked at later.

Assisted-braking devices are, to an extent, auto-locking. They all require a little tension on the dead rope (see Taking-In below) but once they are locked, you can relax a little and do not have to hold the dead rope with any real force. This sounds great, but the disadvantages are significant. The auto-locking system can make it difficult to give slack, they tend to be heavier than tubular devices and they can pretty much only be used with single ropes. They are great for sport climbing but almost useless for multi-pitch and trad routes that require double ropes.

Screw-Gate Carabiner

You need a screw-gate carabiner to attach the belay device, and the rope, to your harness. A screw-gate carabiner is an oval of metal with an opening (gate) that can be locked or unlocked using the threaded barrel (screw). Two key types of carabiner are the D-shaped and pear shaped.

A pear-shaped carabiner is ideal for using with a tubular belay device, as the wide, smooth end lets the rope run easily and the thin end sits neatly on your belay loop. Assisted-braking devices, such as the GRIGRI, often work best with D-shape carabiners, as they help the device to sit in one spot, making cross-loading less likely. A cross-loaded carabiner is one that

GRIGRI 2 setup using a specific carabiner that prevents cross loading.

is loaded side to side rather than top to bottom. Carabiners are significantly weaker in this orientation, though still strong enough for the strains put on them by normal climbing activities. You can buy carabiners specifically designed to be used with your belay device. They generally

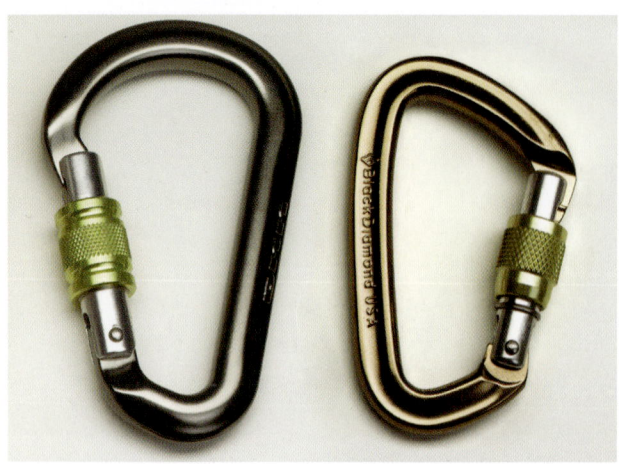

A 'D' and pear-shaped, screw-gate carabiner.

ATC setup using a specific carabiner that prevents cross loading.

TOP ROPING

> **BUYING A BELAY DEVICE**
>
> - Make sure you understand how to use the belay device you are about to buy, or get some instruction on how it works before using it with a live climber.
> - Make sure it is designed for the thickness of rope you are going to be using.
> - Make sure you pair it up with the right type of screw-gate carabiner.

have a mechanism stopping them from spinning around, keeping the carabiner loaded correctly.

Sling 120cm

A sling is a continuous loop of webbing (very strong, flat rope). They come in a variety of lengths (60cm, 120cm and 240cm). They also come in a variety of thicknesses, although they are all pretty much equally strong. The advantage of a very thin sling is that it is lightweight. The disadvantage is that super-thin slings are hard to manipulate, and getting knots out of them can be virtually impossible. They are used in almost all forms of climbing but with indoor top roping they are only used as ground anchors (explained at the bottom of this section). If you only want to go top roping at the wall, and you always climb with people around your own weight, then you probably don't need to buy one. However, if you know that you are likely to climb regularly with someone larger than you, then a 120cm sling and a couple of extra D-shaped screw-gate carabiners would be a wise purchase.

> **BUYING A SLING: AS A GROUND ANCHOR**
>
> - It should be long enough to go from your waist to the floor.
> - Get a medium thickness.
> - Also, buy two small D-shape screw-gate carabiners.

A 120cm sling.

How It All Works

You and your friend pack up your kit and head to the climbing wall. Once you have successfully navigated the reception, café and other distractions, you find yourselves at the bottom of a top-roped route. The rope is already in place running from the bottom of the climb up to the top, through an anchor and back down to the ground. So you have two sides of the same rope at the bottom.

You decide to climb first and tie-in to an end of the rope; your partner attaches the other side of the rope to their harness using the belay device. After a quick check that everything is set up correctly, you start to climb the wall. As you climb, your partner takes in the slack rope. Should you fall off, they are ready to stop you falling any significant distance. Once at the top, your partner will take the rope in tight and, once you have let go, they will lower you back down to the ground. On the ground again, you switch around and it is your friend's turn to climb.

Top Roping Safety Skills

Harnesses

The first harnesses were, literally, a piece of rope wrapped around your waist. Eventually some leg loops where added, purely for comfort, but the waist belt is still the most important bit to get right.

Loosen the Harness Straps and Get Rid of Any Twists It is important that the harness goes on without any twists. This is partly for safety, as a twisted harness cannot be adjusted properly, partly for comfort and partly so as to look like you know what you are doing. A twisted or poorly adjusted harness is the sign of a novice.

Get the Waist Belt Right First The waist belt needs to be above your hips and tightened up so that you cannot get it off without loosening the strap. If your waist belt is too loose, it may creep down with the weight of your kit or, if you did fall in such a way that you inverted, there is a chance you could fall out of it. If your harness requires it, double-back the waist belt buckle now.

> **HARNESS: IN SHORT**
>
> - The waist belt should sit snugly above your hips.
> - Double back if necessary.
> - Keep it neat and tidy.

26 TOP ROPING

Sort the Leg Loops Last Starting with the leg loops will make it harder to get the waist belt to the right height, plus gravity won't be on your side. The leg loops need to be snug but not tight. They want to be comfortable to climb in and also comfortable to hang in when lowering or after a fall.

Tying-In

There are a couple of knots commonly used to attach the climber to the rope. Throughout the book, I will assume the climber uses a rethreaded figure-of-eight with a stopper knot. You may see your friends using a bowline, which is a legitimate method of attachment, but its safety relies wholly on the stopper knot. The stopper knot, when used with a figure-of-eight, is useful as a way to ensure that there is enough tail coming out of the eight to keep it secure. If the stopper knot comes undone, which is does from time to time, there is no need to worry. A bowline, however, is not safe without a stopper knot. If the stopper knot comes undone, which is does from time to time, the safety of the knot is seriously compromised. Below you will find examples of safe and unsafe bowlines for reference, but only the figure-of-eight will be described in full, as I feel this is best practice.

Tying a re-threaded figure-of-eight can be broken down into three skills.

Skill 1: Make the Eight

To tie your rethreaded figure-of-eight, you will need first to create an eight shape in the rope, approximately 1m from the end.

Measure 1m (Approx.) Take the end of the rope in your right hand, and measure to your opposite shoulder, or thereabout. This is where you want your eight to be.

Loops are loose and not twisted.

The waist belt is tight and doubled back.

Finally, the leg loops are tightened and doubled back.

TOP ROPING

GOOD, a perfect re-threaded figure-of-eight with a stopper knot.

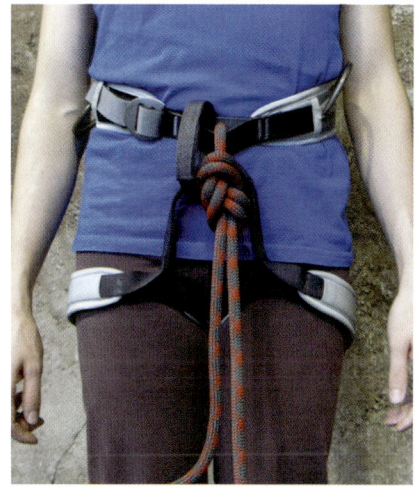
OK, a safe figure-of-eight, even without the stopper knot.

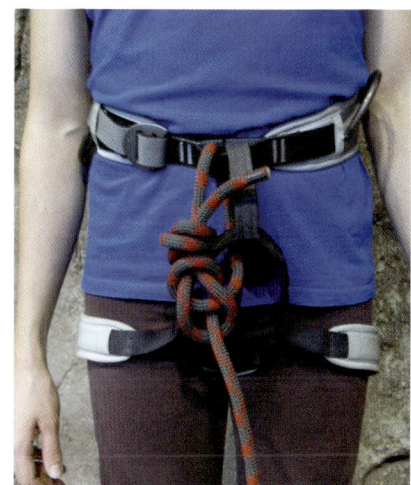
GOOD, a safe bowline, with a stopper knot.

Make a Mountain Holding the rope at the measure point, make a hill or mountain shape away from you (still with the short side of the rope in your right hand).

Make the Face Twist the right side of the mountain over the left side to create a circle (or face) with the short side of the rope on top.

Strangle It Still with your right hand, take the short end of the rope around the back of the face, pulling it tight around the neck.

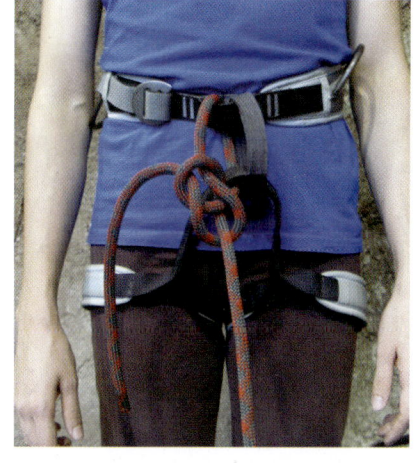
DANGER, a dangerous bowline without a stopper knot.

ABOVE: Measure 1m.

RIGHT: Make a mountain.

28 TOP ROPING

Make a face.

Strangle it.

Poke it in the eye.

Pull it through to make the eight.

GOOD, correctly threaded harness.

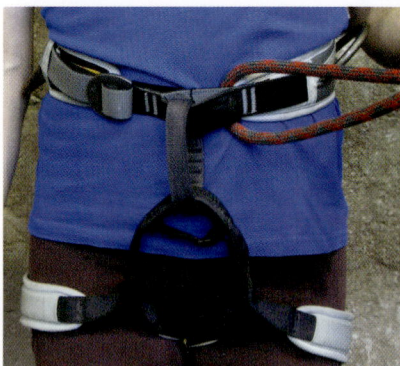

BAD, incorrectly threaded from the top.

DANGER, incorrectly threaded from the bottom.

Poke It In the Eye Take the end of the rope and feed all the excess slack through the circle (or face). You should now have an eight shape in the rope. Make sure it is still around 1m from the end of the rope.

Skill 2: Thread Your Harness
Your harness will have two tie-in loops: one on the leg loops and one on the waist belt. They will have wear webbing around them, which is an extra layer of webbing to stop the rubbing of the rope damaging the load bearing fibres.

These loops can be threaded up or down. It is said that threading down is safer, as if you miss, you are still likely to thread a load-bearing part of your harness. Missing while threading upwards, however, could thread a non load-bearing part of your harness, which could be fatal.

The most important thing is that you check yourself before leaving the ground, as discussed later. Mistakes happen, it is better to always check than to assume that you will be safe because you always thread downwards.

TOP ROPING

Skill 3: Rethreading the Eight
Find the Base Take the end of the rope through the eight, parallel to the rope going directly from the eight to your harness.

Bring it Close Pull all the excess slack through, bringing the eight close to your harness. You want a small loop of rope through your tie-in loops.

Keep to One Side Follow the rest of the eight, keeping the two ropes parallel. Keep to one side, so as to keep it neat.

Dress Your Knot Pull on each of the ropes coming out of your knot individually, so that there are no gaps in the eight. This will make the knot easier to check and ensure that it tightens up evenly when loaded.

Stopper Knot

You need at least 20cm of tail coming out of your well-dressed figure-of-eight, to ensure that the tail will not worm its way back through the eight, and for the knot to be safe. This tail, however, can get in the way while climbing, so we use a stopper knot to clear it away.

Find the base.

Bring it close.

Keep to one side 1.

Keep to one side 2.

Keep to one side 3.

Keep to one side 4.

30 TOP ROPING

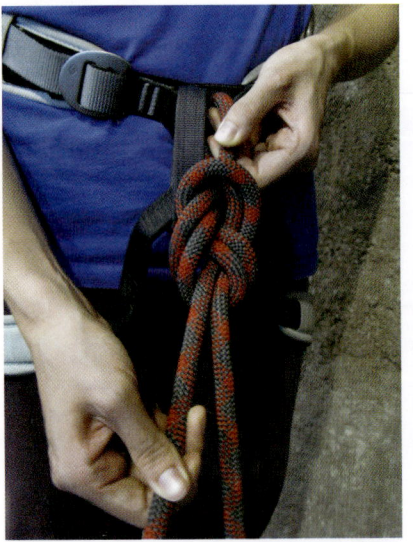

Dress your knot 1.

Dress your knot 2.

Bring Them Parallel The two ropes coming out of the top of the eight are brought next to one another.
Spiral Down Spiral the loose rope down the rope towards the figure-of-eight.
Thread the Hole Thread the end, up through the spiralled rope.
Pull It Down As you pull the end of the rope, making the knot tight, pull the stopper down to meet the figure-of-eight.

MIDDLE LEFT: *Bring them parallel.*

MIDDLE RIGHT: *Spiral down.*

BOTTOM LEFT: *Thread the hole.*

BOTTOM RIGHT: *Pull it down.*

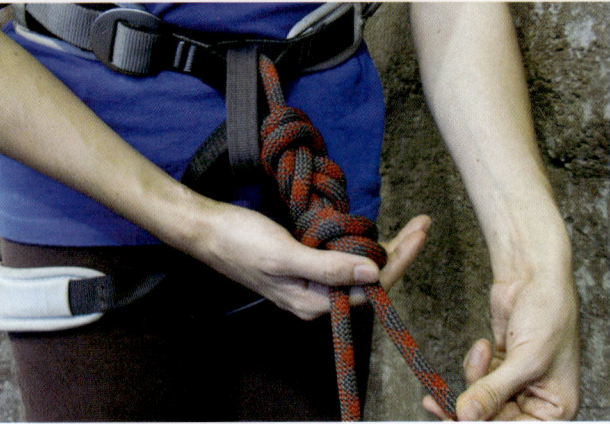

TOP ROPING

> **TYING-IN: IN SHORT**
> - Attach to the right points on the harness.
> - Keep it neat and tidy.

It is important that they live next to each other so as not to make a loop of rope between the figure-of-eight and the stopper. This loop could snag or generally get in the way, particularly when lead climbing.

Belaying

The word belay can mean a variety of things. Here we will discuss belaying from the point of view of a top-rope climber. A belayer is someone who holds your rope while you climb, ensuring that you have sufficient slack to move but, if you fall off, you are held by the rope before you hit the ground. In this sense, belaying is holding the rope for your partner.

For top-rope climbing you need three skills: you need to be able to set up your belay device correctly, take the rope in as your partner climbs and lower them back down the route. All belay devices are slightly different. It is always worth checking the manufacturers' instructions before using your device.

Setting Up Your Tubular Belay Device

Attach It to Your Harness First, it is best to get everything attached to your belay loop in the correct orientation. This means the belay device is the right way round (if it has one) and the screw gate is set with the opening end facing away from you and the screw gate open.

Squeeze the Rope Get a bight of rope through the belay device. The rope now has a live end and a dead end. The live end goes from your belay device to the climber, the dead end goes from your belay device to the floor.

Attach it to your harness.

Squeeze the rope.

32 TOP ROPING

Clip the rope.

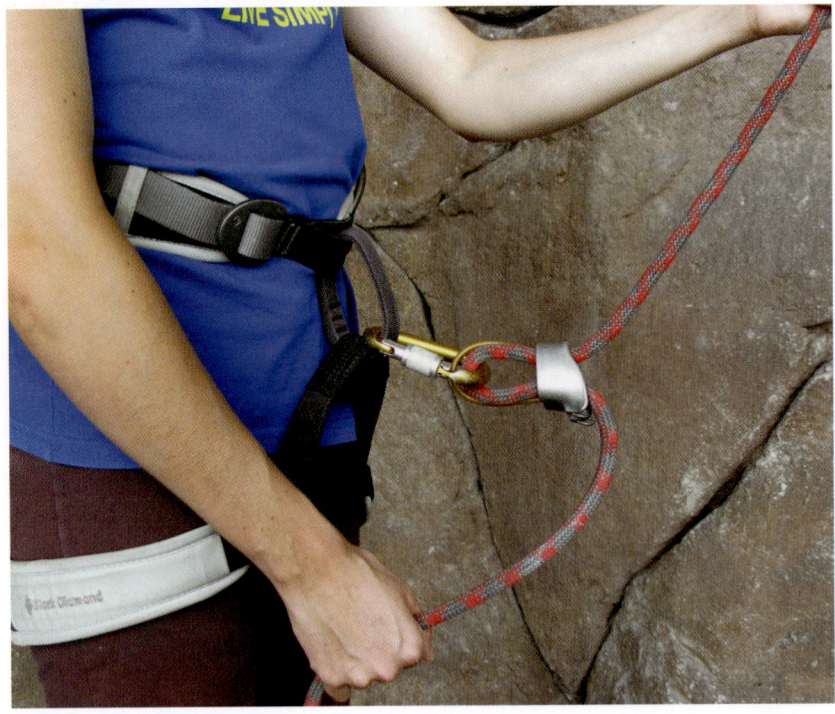

Do up the screw gate.

Clip the Rope The rope should go through the device and then through the screw-gate carabiner. If you have left the gate opening away from you, this should be easy.

Do Up the Screw Gate Make sure the gate closes completely and then screw up the thread.

Setting Up Your Assisted Braking Device (GRIGRI)

Most assisted-braking devices have instructional drawings engraved on the devices themselves. They are all a little different and some are more intuitive than others. Below is a demonstration with a GRIGRI but, if you are using another device, make sure you get some instruction on how to set it up and use it.

Open the GRIGRI Split the GRIGRI in half by pulling back the curved edge

Follow the Arrows Inside there are pictures and arrows indicating where the live and dead ropes come out of the device.

Close the GRIGRI Be sure not to pinch the rope. Once it is closed, you can still check the right rope is coming out of the right hole.

Attach to Your Belay Loop Be sure it is orientated with the handle on top. Clip it to your harness and screw up the carabiner.

Check Each Other Before Climbing: Top Roping

It is vital that you get into the habit of checking your partner before you start climbing. It's something like the buddy system in diving. Even the most experienced climbers in the world can make mistakes.

As a belayer you must check your climber:

- Waist belt – is it tight enough and doubled back if necessary?
- Attachment points – is the knot attached to tie-in loops?
- Knot – is it rethreaded correctly?

TOP ROPING

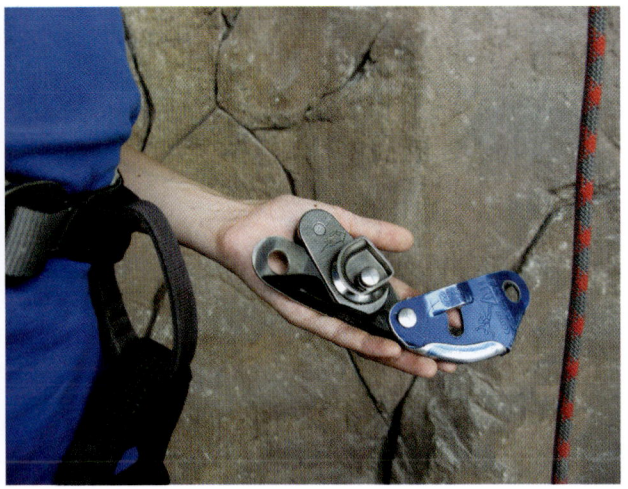
Open the GRIGRI.

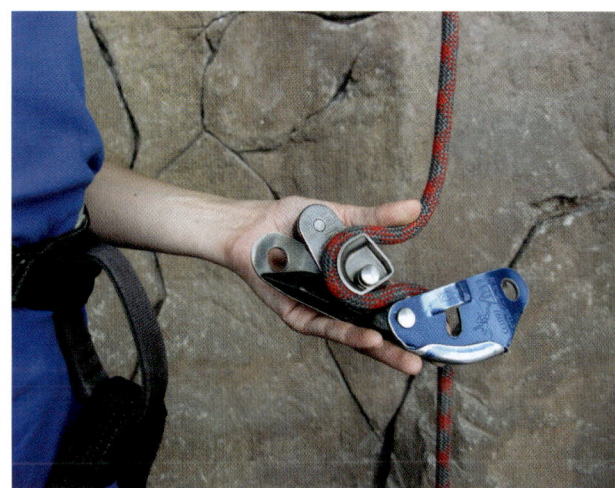
Follow the arrows.

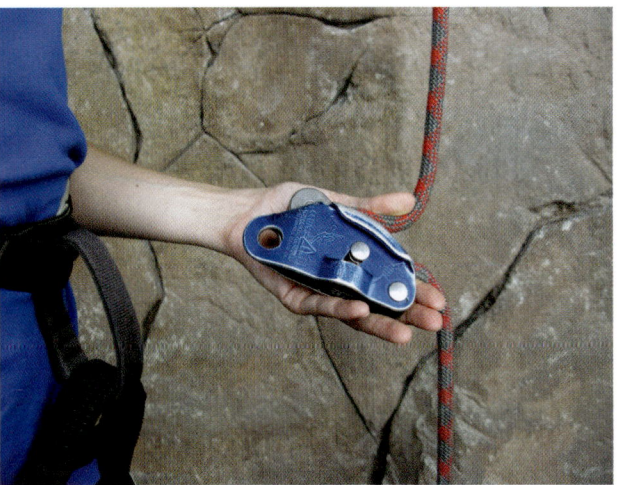
Close the GRIGRI.

Attach to your belay loop.

SETTING UP YOUR BELAY DEVICE: IN SHORT

- Orientate your device first.
- Live rope to the climber.
- Dead rope to the floor.
- Follow the manufacturers' instructions.
- Check each other, before you start climbing.

As a climber you must check your belayer:

- Waist belt – is it tight enough and doubled-back, if necessary?
- Attachment point – is the belay device attached to the belay loop?
- Screw gate – is it done up?

These checks ensure the basic safety chain and will take approximately ten seconds each time. Get into the habit as soon as you can – this is not just a safety precaution but also gives you confidence when pulling hard moves further up your route.

Taking-In

The golden rule with belaying is that you always hold onto the dead rope. The dead rope is the rope that comes out of the device to the ground, as opposed to the live rope that goes up to the climber.

TOP ROPING

Even with an assisted breaking device, such as the GRIGRI, the following system should be used, as these devices require a little tension on the dead rope in order to lock effectively.

The easy way to remember the taking-in system is to use the rhyme: V to the knee, one, two, three.

Start/Stop Point This is your default position when top-rope belaying. This is a locked-off position that essentially means that it will be simple to hold the rope, should your climber fall off. For this demonstration I will talk about right-handed belaying, but it is the same method if you need to do it left-handed.

Your right hand is on the dead rope a few inches from the belay device; your left hand is high on the live rope. There is a little tension in the whole system, which allows you to feel what is going on with your climber. We call this top hand the pulse hand. You should be able to feel when your climber is about to move by feeling the tension change on the live rope.

V As your climber moves up the wall, the rope will become slack. So, you need to pull this excess rope through your belay device. Bring your right hand (still holding the dead rope) out of the locked position and pull the rope up through the device. Your top hand will gently assist the live rope down.

To the Knee The V position is obviously not a position to hang around in, as the device is no longer locked. So, as soon as an armful of slack has come through the device, you bring your right hand down, somewhere near your knee. The device is now locked again. However, we need to return to the original position (without dropping the dead rope) to be able to take in multiple times.

One Bring your top (left) hand down to the dead rope just below the belay device.

Two Now, as the dead rope is secured by your left hand, you can bring your right hand back to its original position.

Three As the dead rope is secured by your right hand, you can finally move your left hand back, high on the live rope, to its original position, feeling for changes in tension from your climber.

> **TAKING-IN: IN SHORT**
> - Always hold onto the dead rope.
> - V to the knee, one, two, three.
> - The top hand, is the pulse hand.

Start/stop point.

V.

TOP ROPING 35

To the knee.

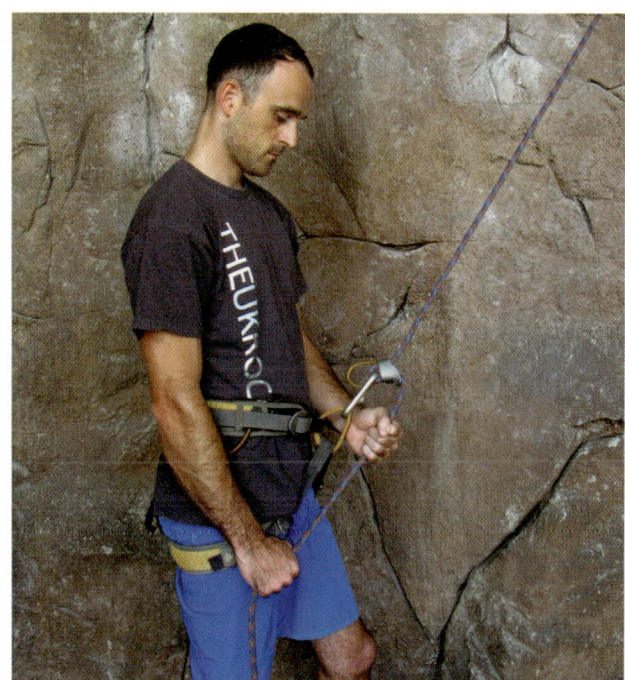

One.

Two.

Three.

36 TOP ROPING

Lower the climber 1.

Lower the climber 2.

Lower the climber 3.

Lowering With Tubular Devices

Once your climber reaches the top, it is normal for them to be lowered back to the ground, as apposed to climbing back down. This can be a daunting prospect for the climber; it requires great trust in their belayer. It is important that you develop trust by using good communication and understanding.

Climber Arrives at the Top As the climber arrives at the final holds, they will indicate that they are finished. Some use a thumbs up, others will say 'OK' or 'finished' or something along those lines. The main thing is that you recognize, as a belayer, that your climber is ready to be lowered.

Take In Tight It is comforting for the climber if the rope is taken in tight before they lean back. The ropes we use have an inherent stretch to them, so if the rope is slightly slack, the climber will drop a few feet before the rope becomes tight, which can be scary. Once you have taken the rope tight, you put both hands onto the dead rope.

The Climber Lets Go Once they are happy that you have taken their weight, they will let go. It is really important that you keep them suspended at the top for a few seconds to allow them to get into a good position to be lowered and to trust their weight to you completely.

Lower the Climber Your top hand stays rigidly a few inches away from your device. It is best to place it at the height of, and touching, your belay loop. Your bottom hand then feeds rope into the top hand in a smooth motion until the climber is back on the ground.

A common accident involves the top hand getting too close to the belay device. As the rope is moving into the device, it will easily pull some skin in with it, causing pain and, in some cases, real damage. If this happens, you need to get your climber to lift their weight off the rope for a second so you can release your hand, but it is obviously best avoided, by keeping your top hand against your belay loop.

Lowering With Assisted Braking Device (GRIGRI)

GRIGRIs, and other assisted-braking devices, have an inherent problem with lowering. They are set up to lock as soon as any weight is applied to the live rope. You are forced to disable the device in order to bring your climber down.

You must keep control of the dead rope while disabling the locking

Lowering with a GRIGRI.

TOP ROPING

> **LOWERING: IN SHORT**
> - Take in tight.
> - Ensure the climber has let go.
> - Lower slowly, with your top hand against your belay loop.
> - Always keep control of the dead rope.

mechanism. With most devices, the disabling handle is catastrophically on or off, and even one second with your hand only on the handle, will see your climber free fall to the ground.

Keeping one hand on the dead rope, the other hand gently pulls back on the handle. Once the locking mechanism is disabled sufficiently, you can let the dead rope slide slowly through your hand into the device. If you need them to stop, you simply let go of the handle, enabling the locking mechanism to take control again. Always keep hold of the dead rope.

Ground Anchoring

If you weigh significantly less than your partner (a difference of 20kg or more), you may wish to anchor yourself to the floor when belaying, to make sure you do not leave the ground when they fall off. There are various methods of ground anchoring in a climbing wall. Some walls will have ballast bags (sacks full of sand) that have a daisy chain (a length of small slings linked together) on them, which you simply clip to yourself at the right height. Some will have bags but no daisy chains, and some have bolts attached to the floor, which you need to attach to using a sling or the rope.

For top roping I will explain, in detail, a method using a sling and two carabiners. The most important thing to get right with a ground anchor system is to make sure that 'ABC' are in line, as explained below.

GOOD, ABC is in line, so any fall will have little impact on the belayer.

BAD, standing behind the ground anchor will pull the belayer forward if the climber falls off.

38 TOP ROPING

BAD, a loose setup will pull the belayer into the air before the ground anchor takes effect.

Clip in.

Anchor, Belayer, Climber (ABC)

When the climber falls off, and their weight is applied to the belayer, ABC will come into line. That is the Anchor, the Belay device and the Climber (or in this case the anchor at the top of the wall), will try their best to become an exact straight line. If you set up your system already in a straight line, then when they fall off, it will all be very comfortable. If your setup is not in a straight line (for instance, standing behind the anchor or with a loose sling to the floor), then when they fall off, you will be forced into that straight line, whether you like it or not.

Ground Anchors: One Sling, Two Carabiners

Clip In The sling needs to be attached to yourself, with one carabiner, and to the ground anchor with the other.

Tighten It Up Take one side of the sling and put an overhand knot in it to shorten the main section of the sling. It is tight enough when it pulls you down gently, when your back foot is up against the anchor.

> **GROUND ANCHORS: IN SHORT**
> - ABC in line.
> - No slack in the system.
> - Back foot against the anchor.

> **JARGON**
>
> **Climbing wall:** indoor climbing gym.
> **Cross-loading:** a carabiner loaded side to side, which is much weaker than loading top to bottom.
> **Anchor:** any solid point which a climber uses to attach themselves to the rock or the ground.

Stand on the Correct Side If you are belaying right-handed, then your right foot needs to be up against the anchor. This will leave enough room for your right arm to belay effectively. If you have your left foot against the anchor, and your right foot forward, your right arm will be impeded.

TOP ROPING 39

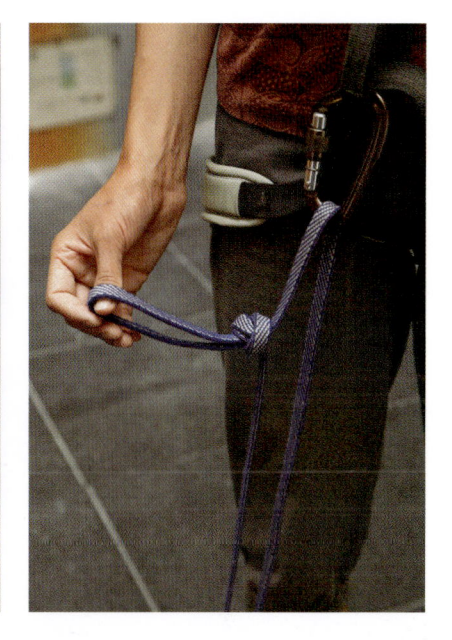

Tighten it up 1.

Tighten it up 2.

Tighten it up 3.

LEFT: GOOD, right foot back for right-hand belaying.

RIGHT: BAD, left foot back for right-hand belaying.

CHAPTER 9

SPORT CLIMBING

Michael Stevenson ready to clip a lower-off in the Gorge du Tarn. © STEVE GORTON

Sport Climbing Kit List

Shoes

See Chapter 7 for climbing shoe details.

Chalk and Chalk Bag

See Chapter 7 for details of chalk and chalk bags.

Harness

See Chapter 8 for details of harnesses.

Belay Device and Screw-Gate Carabiner

See Chapter 8 for details on belay devices and screw gates.

Quickdraws

Quickdraws are used to clip the rope to the bolts when you are climbing. A quickdraw consists of two carabiners linked together with a small piece of webbing. The carabiners are not screw-gated and are usually called snap links.

Sport climbing quickdraws should be short, fat and have a smooth nose. Short, so that they do not swing around on your

> **BUYING QUICKDRAWS: FOR SPORT CLIMBING**
>
> - Short and fat is best.
> - Key lock snap-links are ideal.
> - Twelve should get you started.

SPORT CLIMBING

Snap link with a hooked nose.

Short, fat quickdraws for sport climbing.

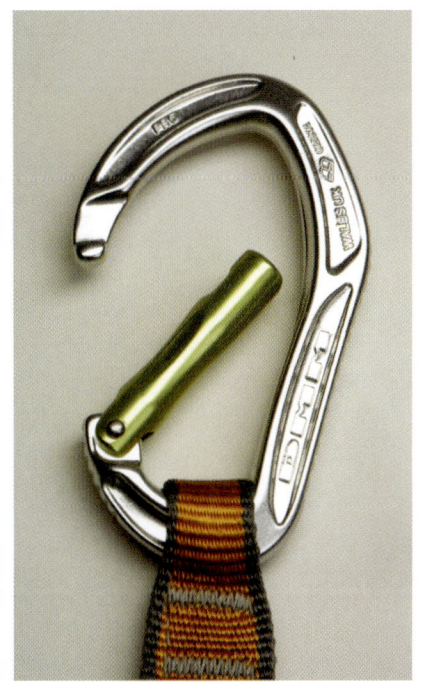

harness or in the wind while you are trying to clip them. Fat, so that you can hold onto them, using them like extra holds on the rock, while you work your route. The nose of the snap link is the point where the gate opens and closes. Some use a small hook in the nose to hold the gate in place, but this hook can be annoying when you are trying to unclip the quickdraw from your harness, rope or bolt. Key lock snap-links have smooth noses, removing this issue.

You will need at least one quickdraw for every bolt on the route and one for the lower-off. For some very long routes, you may need sixteen or more, but for most routes, twelve is sufficient. When sport climbing indoors, most walls will have the quickdraws pre-placed.

Cow's Tail

A cow's tail is used to attach yourself to

Snap links with key lock systems are less likely to snag.

RIGHT: *Cow's tail setup using one 60cm sling, lark's footed directly to the belay loop with a small 'D'-shaped carabiner.*

42 SPORT CLIMBING

> **BUYING A COW'S TAIL**
>
> - One 60cm sling.
> - One small D-shaped screw-gate carabiner.

the lower-off while you rethread your rope ready to be lowered. The ideal cow's tail is made using a 60cm sling and a small D-shaped carabiner. The sling is attached to your harness by passing the sling through itself, around the belay loop. This knot is called a lark's foot.

Rope

Ropes for sport climbing come in diameters of approximately 9 to 11mm, with thinner ropes being lighter but potentially harder to handle when belaying.

Your rope must be at least twice as long as your route. If you are at a climbing wall that is 15m high, then you need at least a 30m rope, as your climber needs to get to the top and then be lowered back to the ground. Outdoor sports routes can have pitches of up to 40m long, with the majority being under 30m. Ropes usually come in lengths of 35, 50, 60 or 70m, although a few 80m plus ropes are on the market.

Another feature to consider is dry treatment. Manufacturers dry treat ropes to stop moisture from getting into them and basically make them last longer. Dry-treated ropes are usually more expensive than those that are not, so it is worth thinking about where the rope will mostly be used. Ropes that will only be used indoors do not require dry

> **BUYING A ROPE: FOR SPORT CLIMBING**
>
> - Make sure your rope will be long enough for the routes you intend to climb.
> - Consider dry-treated ropes for outdoor climbing.
> - Separate indoor/outdoor ropes, if you do both regularly.
> - Using a ground sheet will increase the life of your rope.

treatment, but it will be useful if you plan to climb outdoors in Britain.

If you are going to sport climb indoors and outdoors, then it is recommended to buy two ropes. Using your 70m rope regularly on a 15m wall pushes all the fibres into the middle section of the rope. This makes the rope get fat and twisted in the middle, which ruins it. It would be better to get one 35m rope for your twice weekly trips to the wall and a 70m for your weekend trips to the crag.

Rope bags are very basic bags with an integral ground sheet that can be laid down, underneath your rope, to stop it from getting dirty. Ropes have a habit of picking up sand and other dirt that then gets into the core and starts to break up the fibres. If you always keep your rope off the ground this will happen far more slowly, increasing the life of your rope.

Helmets

Helmets were originally designed only to protect you from falling rocks. Their hard plastic shells were made to deflect blows from above. Modern helmets are designed to provide protection from this

A brand new 70m sport rope.

SPORT CLIMBING

A suspension and a foam helmet.

as well as side impact you could sustain if you hit your head while falling off your route.

There are basically two types of helmet on the market: suspension and foam. Suspension helmets have a hard outer shell and a separate inner cradle. They use the same deflecting system mentioned above, but also absorb some of the force, rather than transferring it straight into the climber's head and neck. These are a common choice for alpine climbers and beginners, as they are very durable.

Foam helmets have a very thin shell around hardened foam. They absorb impact forces from all directions but are one-hit wonders. Once they have taken a hit, they have to be retired straight away. Being lightweight, they are a common choice for trad and sport climbers.

A good helmet for you should fit well before you do up the chinstrap. It should be snug around the back of your head and above your eyebrows. Ideally, you will not be able to see it too much in your peripheral vision. If you mainly climb on hot summer days, then you will be looking for as much ventilation as you can get. A winter climber, however, may be more interested to know if they can get a hat on underneath.

To Wear It or Not To Wear It?

You will see plenty of people not wearing helmets and, depending on the venue, this can be a reasonable decision. A steep, relatively short, popular crag is less likely to shed loose rocks than a massive 500m face in the Alps, where ice melting and freezing loosens the rock.

In terms of hitting your head during a fall, you are more likely to get into trouble on easy, angled routes where a fall could be more of a tumble. Getting your leg trapped behind the rope, as we shall see later, could result in the climber inverting while they fall, which could also lead to head injury. Helmets are generally lightweight and comfortable these days, so the excuses for not wearing one are running thin. However, they can hinder your performance slightly, particularly in hot weather. It is best to take every venue's objective dangers into account before deciding whether to put on or take off your helmet.

> **HELMETS: IN SHORT**
>
> - If your crag is large, slabby or loose, then a helmet is essential.

44 SPORT CLIMBING

> **BUYING A HELMET**
> - Get the right helmet for your main style of climbing.
> - Make sure your peripheral vision is not impaired.
> - A comfy helmet is worn more often.

How It All Works

You and your friend pack up your kit along with lunch and head to the crag. After finding your route, you unpack the kit, rack up and flake out the rope (remembering to put a knot in the bottom end, as will be discussed later). You decide you are climbing first, so you tie-in to the top end of the rope and your partner attaches their belay device to the rope a few metres down the rope from you.

After a quick check, you start up the wall. The route has bolts periodically all the way to the top and you clip the rope to them with quickdraws as you climb. Your partner gives you enough slack to climb but is prepared to hold you should you fall off. Once you arrive at the top, you clip the lower-off with a quickdraw and get lowered down the route.

Now it is your friend's turn to climb. The difference this time is that the quickdraws are already in place (you kindly left them there for your partner to use). On arriving at the top, your partner will clip themselves in and thread the lower-off. This allows them to be lowered down the climb, retrieving all the quickdraws, leaving the route as you found it. Back on the ground, after several high fives and much rejoicing, you and your friend choose another route and start again.

Sport Climbing Safety Skills

Advanced at the Basics

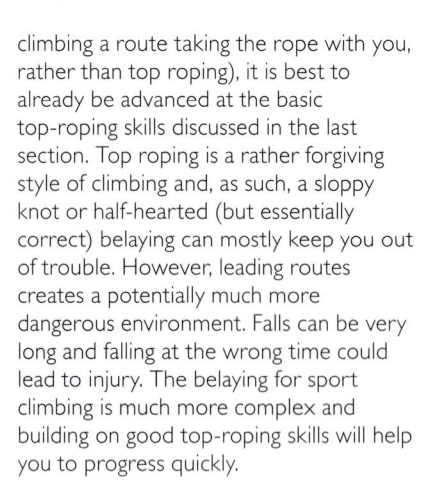

Before starting to lead routes (that is, climbing a route taking the rope with you, rather than top roping), it is best to already be advanced at the basic top-roping skills discussed in the last section. Top roping is a rather forgiving style of climbing and, as such, a sloppy knot or half-hearted (but essentially correct) belaying can mostly keep you out of trouble. However, leading routes creates a potentially much more dangerous environment. Falls can be very long and falling at the wrong time could lead to injury. The belaying for sport climbing is much more complex and building on good top-roping skills will help you to progress quickly.

Basic 1: Harness

Be sure it is above your hips. Wearing your harness below your hips increases the chance of inverting during a fall. If you are at all unsure, make sure you re-read the top rope section on harnesses.

Basic 2: Tying-In

When lead climbing, you need to be able to reach past your knot to get hold of live rope quickly when clipping. A good test is as follows: tie-in as normal, then without bending your back, reach down past your knot and get hold of the rope below. If you cannot reach past the knot, either your knot needs to be neatened and tightened (bringing it closer to your harness) or your waist belt needs bringing up a little.

If you do not pass this test, it will mean that when you are hanging on (for dear life), you will have to spend an extra few seconds looking for the rope that you need to clip. Times this by every bolt and that is a lot of energy to burn for no good reason. Make sure you re-read the top rope section on tying-in, if you are at all unsure.

Basic 3: Belaying

When somebody falls off on top rope, the forces involved are pretty insignificant, as the rope is above them the whole time. When someone falls off from above their last bolt (when lead climbing), the forces generated before the weight is transferred to the belayer are much more significant.

GOOD, this knot is close to the harness and will leave the rope free when leading.

BAD, this knot is too large and will hinder your climbing performance when leading.

SPORT CLIMBING

> **ADVANCED AT THE BASICS: IN SHORT**
> - It is advisable to be a solid top-roper before moving on to leading.
> - Make sure your knots are neat and tidy.
> - Calm, confident top-rope belaying is a good launching point for lead belaying.

A belayer must be prepared for this change.

Also, the belayer needs to be able to adjust the slack in the system quickly and safely, depending on the climber's movements. On occasion, the climber may ask (in quite a stressful tone) for the rope to be taken in; a good belayer needs to be able to calmly but quickly take in this slack without compromising the technique demonstrated in the top roping chapter.

Prep: Sport Climbing

Before starting up your route, you will need to get ready. If you are the climber, you will rack up, which means you get all the equipment you will need on the route onto your harness in a neat and ordered fashion. As a general rule, have the things you will need while climbing at the front (quickdraws) and things you will need at the belays and lower-offs at the back (carabiners, slings, prusiks).

The belayer will flake out the rope, piling it up onto itself. As they do this, they will be checking for abrasions, unwanted knots and that the rope will lift off the top of the rope pile smoothly. The belayer should also put a knot in the bottom end of the rope, just in case the rope is not long enough for the route.

This knot in the bottom of the rope is a life-saver. Many people have been caught out climbing a 35m route on a 60m rope only to lower-off and find they are 10m short of the ground. If the belayer doesn't notice, they may let the rope go all the way through the device and the climber will fall 10m to the floor. This happens all too regularly, so make sure you put a knot in the bottom of the rope every time.

A well-racked harness ready to lead a sport route.

The knot in the bottom of the rope is a life-saver.

Flaking the rope while checking for knots and abrasions.

Check Each Other Before Climbing: Sport Climbing

It is vital that you get into the habit of checking your partner before you start climbing. It's something like the buddy system in diving. Even the most experienced climbers in the world can make mistakes.

As a belayer you must check your climber:

- Waist belt – is it tight enough and doubled-back, if necessary?
- Attachment points – is the knot attached to the tie-in loops?
- Knot – is it rethreaded correctly?
- Knot – is there one in the bottom end of the rope?

As a climber you must check your belayer:

- Waist belt – is it tight enough and doubled back if necessary?
- Attachment point – is the belay device attached to the belay loop?
- Screw gate – is it done up?
- Knot – is there one in the bottom end of the rope?

These checks ensure the basic safety chain and will take approximately ten seconds each time. Get into the habit as soon as you can. This is not just a safety precaution but also gives you confidence when pulling hard moves further up your route.

Leading Basics

As a leader (rather than a top-roper), you will have to climb up the wall, clipping quickdraws into the wall and the rope into these quickdraws. When you get to the end of your climb, you need to be able to re-thread the lower-off. At the top of lead routes indoors, there are normally two bolts linked together with a chain and a handy carabiner for you to clip into and be lowered from. Outdoors, however, an in situ carabiner would get rusty and the gate would become unusable. Instead, solid rings with no gates are used. You will come across various setups, all requiring you to be able to safely untie and thread your rope through a smooth metal ring, tie back in and be lowered.

As a lead belayer (rather than a top-rope belayer), the extra skill required is to be able to give slack to your climber. Some practice will mean you can move easily and efficiently, from giving to taking, without ever breaking the golden rule (always hold onto the dead rope). A good lead belayer will be aware of the advantages of dynamic belaying, and will also be able to help their climber avoid certain dangers, as will be discussed later.

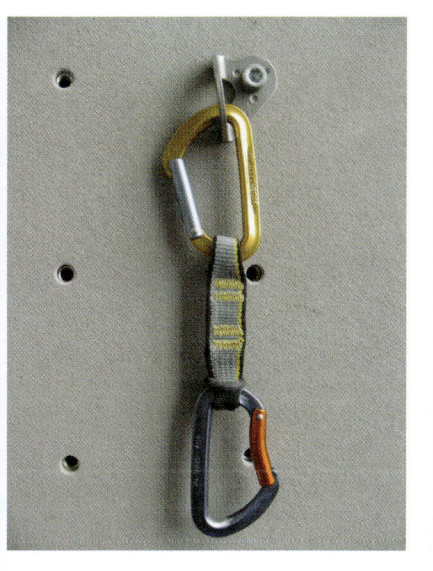

SPORT CLIMBING 47

GOOD, quickdraw in the correct orientation.

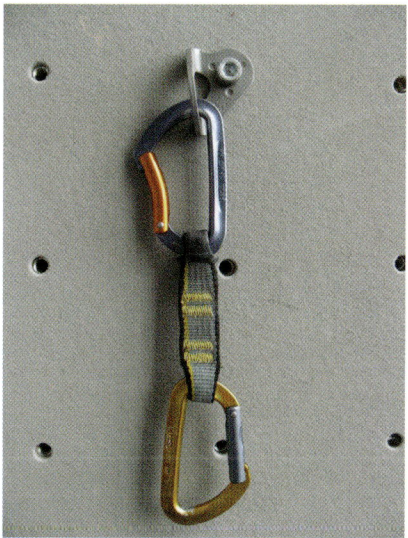

BAD, quickdraw in the wrong orientation.

The top snap link is knarled from hanging on bolts.

The bottom snap link has been smoothed out by the rope.

GOOD, this is a correct clip.

DANGER, this is a back clip and could come undone in a fall.

Clipping the Quickdraw to the Bolt

Quickdraws come with a top and bottom end. The top snap-link will have a straight gate and will be loosely held in the webbing. The bottom snap-link will be tightly attached to the webbing, normally with some sort of rubber band, to stop it from turning upside down. It is important to always use your quickdraws the correct way round, partly as they are designed, and therefore easier to use, this way round. But also because the snap link that goes to the bolt will get churned up far more quickly than the rope end. This constant abuse the top snap link gets can create small ridges and spikes that can damage the rope if it runs over them with any force. The bottom snap-link will always have the rope running through it and will therefore be extremely smooth and rope-friendly.

Clipping the Rope to the Quickdraw

There is a right and wrong way for the rope to run through the quickdraw. The wrong way is called a 'back clip' and can

48 SPORT CLIMBING

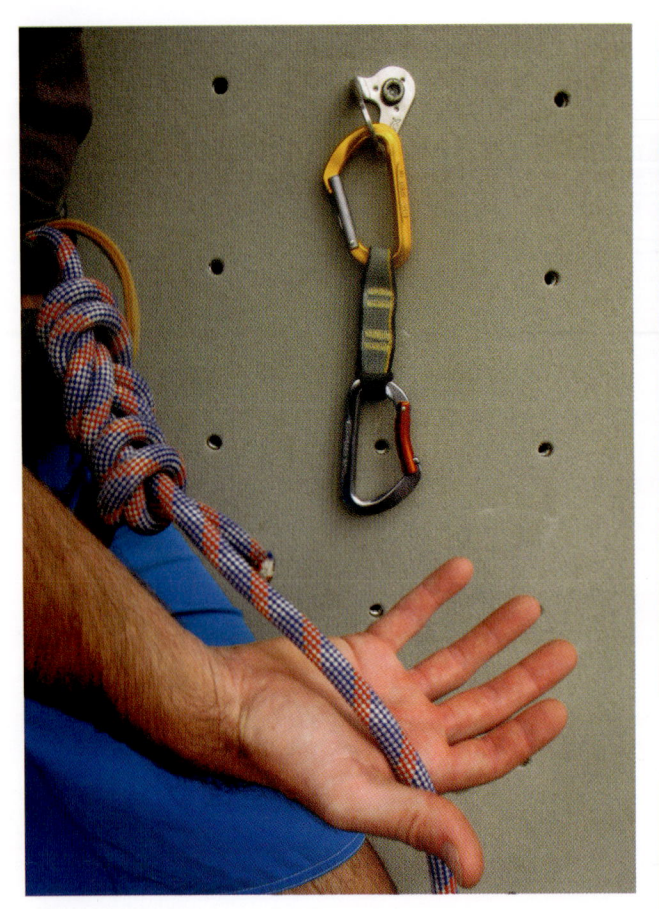

Find the rope.

Bring up slack.

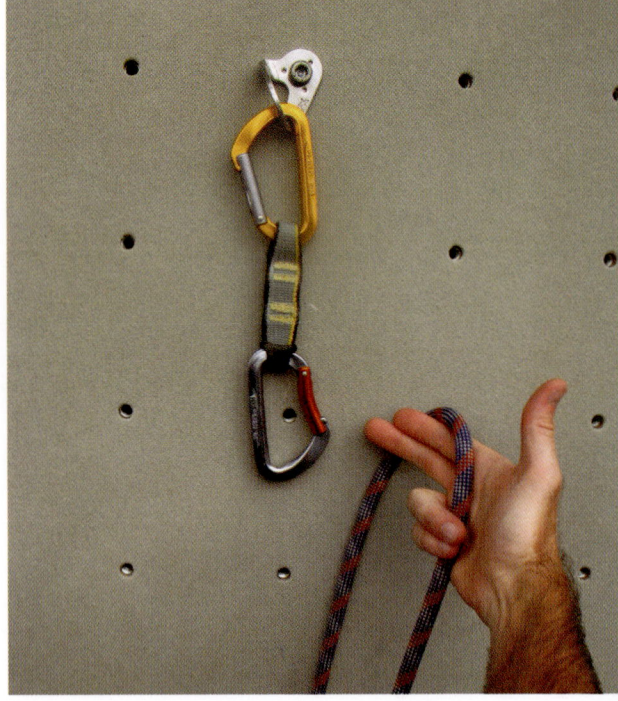

Make the gun.

lead to the rope coming out of the quickdraw during a fall (this will be looked at in detail in the next section). The correct way for the rope to run through the quickdraw is so that the rope leading up to you comes out from the wall, or to put it another way, the rope goes from your knot and dives into the snap gate, towards the wall.

How you get the rope into the snap link is up to you. I will outline a couple of techniques below, but however you choose to clip, make sure you can do it quickly, from all angles, with either hand and with certainty.

Method 1: Gun Method
Find the Rope Reach down and take the rope with your palm facing outwards.

Bring Up Slack Bring up enough slack to comfortably get the rope into the snap link. If the rope is heavy, it may be necessary to use your mouth to help bring it up in stages. All climbers do this from time to time but a few have fallen off and lost teeth in the process, so be warned.

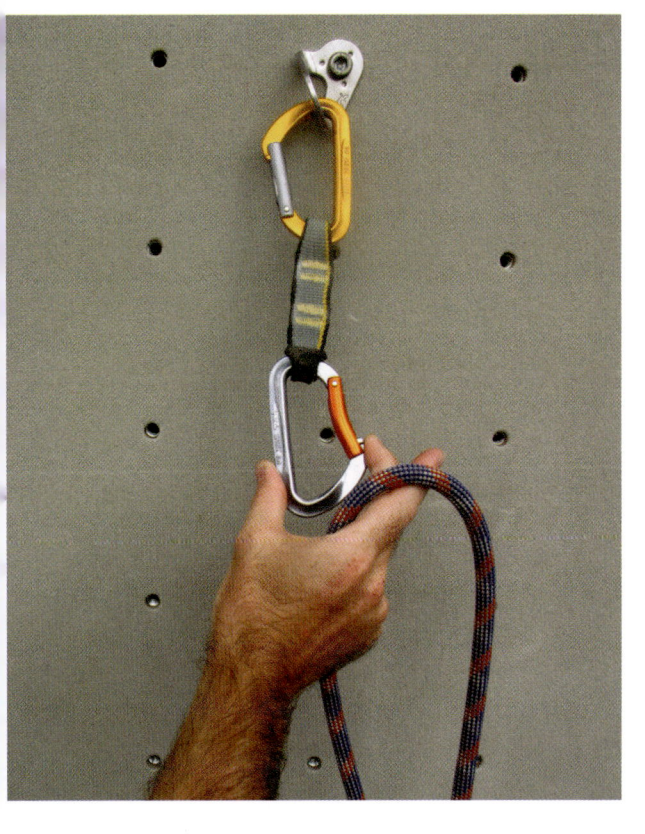

SPORT CLIMBING

Hold the snap link.

Clip the rope in.

Make the Gun Bring your third and little finger to your palm, holding the rope. The rope now runs from your knot, between your palm and these fingers, up over your index finger (or gun) and down to the belayer.

Hold the Snap Link Use your middle finger and thumb to hold the quickdraw steady.

Clip the Rope In Flick the rope over the top of your hand onto the bent gate of the snap link. Tilt the snap link up to allow gravity to help you press the rope through the gate. This method is also called the forehand method (as in tennis). It may seem like a lot of steps but with practice it should take about one second to perform. This will work with the left hand when the gate faces left or with the right hand when the gate faces right.

Method 2: Tea with the Queen
Find the Rope Reach down and take the rope with your palm facing outwards.

Bring Up Slack Bring up enough slack to comfortably get the rope into the snap link.

Tea with the Queen Turn your hand over so that the rope falls into, and is pinched by, your index finger and thumb; your remaining fingers extend into the air (as though you where holding a tea cup, across from the Queen).

Hold the Snap Link Hang your middle finger in the base of the snap link to hold it steady.

Clip the Rope In Pull in slightly with your middle finger, while turning the gate towards you. Push the rope through with your index finger and thumb. When practising, make sure you are still holding the rope once it has gone all the way through. A common mistake is to let go too early, leaving the rope caught in the gate. This method is also called the backhand method (as in tennis). It will work with the left hand when the gate faces right or with the right hand when the gate faces left.

With these two methods you should be able to clip pretty much any quickdraw in any orientation. There are plenty of other ways to achieve the same thing, so watch other climbers and be willing to give their methods a go (maybe theirs will suit you better). It will take a little practice to be clipping well, and it is worth getting good at it, as fumbling clips can be very frustrating. Try focusing on good clipping technique on your warm-up routes, so that you are ready to get the rope in, quick as a flash, on your hardest routes of the day.

50 SPORT CLIMBING

Find the rope.

Bring up slack.

Tea with the Queen.

Hold the snap link.

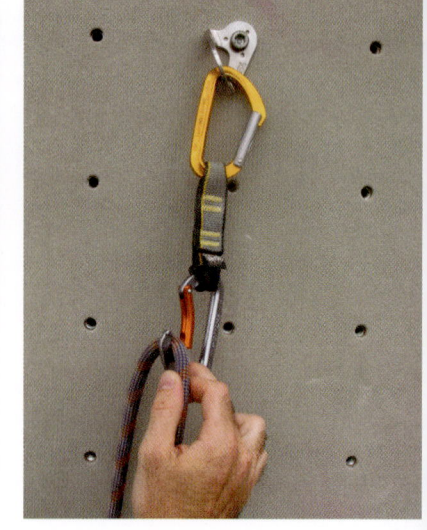

Clip the rope in.

SPORT CLIMBING

> **CLIPPING: IN SHORT**
> - Orientate the quickdraw correctly.
> - Avoid back clipping.
> - Practice makes perfect.

Giving Slack

The golden rule with belaying is that you never let go of the dead rope. The dead rope is the rope that comes out of the device to the ground, as apposed to the live rope that goes up to your climber. This rule does not change for lead belaying.

Giving Slack With Tubular Devices

The following is a breakdown of how to give slack with a tubular device. It is a one, two, three method that is simple and gives us the foundation for dynamic belaying, as will be shown a little later in this chapter.

Start/Stop Point This is your default position when lead belaying. You are ready to give slack and you are in a locked-off position, which means that it will be simple to hold a fall should your climber fall off. For this demonstration I will talk about right-handed belaying, but it is the same principle if you need to do it left-handed. The whole system needs to be loose. If you are holding the rope tightly through the belay device, it will not move smoothly.

One Bring your right hand (still holding the rope) to touch your hip, while your left hand pulls an armful of slack through the device. Where your right hand ends up is very important. If it gets too close to the device when the climber falls off, the rope may drag your hand (or skin) into the device. Make a point of always touching your hip (between your waist belt and leg loops) every time you give slack. This will become important when dynamic belaying.

Two Let go with your left hand and then hold the rope just above the belay device. It is important to hold the rope up so that the belay device gently pulls up on

Start/stop point.

One.

Two.

Three.

your belay loop, to allow the next move (three) to be completed effectively.

Three Under the tension created by your left hand holding the rope up, slide your right hand back down the dead rope. You should then be able to get your right hand a long way back from the device, ready to give out a good amount of slack on the next set. It is important that when you slide your right hand down you are *still holding the dead rope*. You slide it back under tension, still with your whole hand around, and touching the rope. You *cannot* reverse this process and slide your hand up the rope, as there is no tension from the other end, which would force you to let go (breaking the golden rule).

Giving Slack With a GRIGRI
The GRIGRI, and other assisted-braking devices, can be difficult to use for lead belaying. They are set up to lock as soon as any tension comes from the live rope. Unfortunately, this can mean that when you try to give slack to your climber, the device can lock up. Below I will give you a quick breakdown of how a GRIGRI works and four options for giving slack, but always read the manufacturer's instructions for your particular device.

Inside a GRIGRI The moving part of a GRIGRI is a pivoting cam. This cam relies on friction from the rope to pivot the top of the cam upwards, forcing the bottom of the cam to pinch the rope tight. The more upward force, the more it pinches. Keeping the ropes coming into and out of the GRIGRI, as close to parallel as possible, reduces the friction and the GRIGRI is less likely to pinch the rope, unless there is a major force (or fall).

Method 1 Your left hand gently pulls live rope out of the GRIGRI. Your right hand keeps the dead rope vertically above the GRIGRI, keeping the two ropes parallel while you feed the rope through the device.

Method 2 This is the same as using a tubular belay device. Make sure you keep the dead rope running over the curved edge of the GRIGRI, otherwise the device is sure to lock up at inopportune moments.

SPORT CLIMBING

Inside a GRIGRI when unlocked.

Inside a GRIGRI when locked.

Method 3 Fold the dead rope over the curved edge. The dead rope runs through your right hand with your first finger placed under the curved edge, lifting up the GRIGRI. In this position the live rope can be pulled out of the device quite sharply, while still having a hand around the dead rope and without interfering with the device's camming action.

Method 4 If the rope jams, it becomes necessary to forcibly unlock the device to pull rope through. Get the GRIGRI set up exactly as in method three but this time put your thumb over the handle and squeeze it open. Once it is open, you can pull rope through as fast as you like. Be aware that with your thumb over the handle, the device is completely disabled. There have been incidents where belayers have kept their thumb on the handle when their climber has fallen off, resulting in the climber free-falling to the ground before the belayer was able to react. Only use this method if the other methods have failed, and only briefly disable the camming action of the device.

Give, Take, Give, Give a Bit More, Take... When belaying a lead climber, you need to be constantly monitoring the amount of slack in the system. You may need to give rope one second, take it the next and give again afterwards. Moving between giving and taking slack takes a little practice. Try using a top rope and get your partner to climb up and down the wall at random. You constantly keep the rope close but not tight, thus having to give and take as they climb up and down.

One of the simplest ways to give and take rope quickly is to walk towards or away from the base of the route. People often find it difficult to give enough slack when the climber requires it very quickly. A step towards the wall can give a metre or so of slack before you have started to move your hands. This technique is only

54 SPORT CLIMBING

practical when you have a flat area to walk across, as tripping up may be dangerous for the climber.

Think about what you need when you are lead climbing. The last thing you want is to be pulled off because your belayer will not give you the slack you need. On the other hand, you do not want to fall too far if you fall off. So, basically, you want the rope to be loose enough to move, but close enough to keep you safe.

> **LEAD BELAYING: IN SHORT**
> - Always hold onto the dead rope.
> - Keep the rope loose, but safe.
> - Taking-in: V to the knee, one, two, three.
> - Giving slack: one, two, three.

Giving slack with a GRIGRI: method two.

Giving slack with a GRIGRI: method one.

Giving slack with a GRIGRI: method three.

SPORT CLIMBING

LEFT: Giving slack with a GRIGRI: method four.

A para bolt and chain lower-off.

A good tat lower-off.

Lower-Offs

Lower-Off Types
At the top of your sport route you will find a lower-off. Lower-offs come in a variety of styles (some better than others). Generally there will be two bolts linked together with a chain and a ring on the chain.

Sometimes the bolts will be linked together with old tat (generic term of old cut-offs of rope or sling), which is less than ideal as it degrades quickly when left out in the elements. You will have to judge the quality of the tat carefully and leave behind a spare snap-link on the bolts, if necessary. It is really important to remember to make sure your rope is running over a smooth metal part of the lower-off (such as a ring, mallion or carabiner). If you were to thread the rope directly over the tat (fabric on fabric), the heat generated while lowering-off will almost certainly cause the rope to melt through the tat.

Sometimes there will just be two bolts that you thread directly; these must be glue-in bolts that have smooth edges or have a mallion or ring through them. Bolts with square edges (expansion bolts) must not be threaded. Threading square-sided bolts could cut your rope as you are lowered.

The quality of bolts and lower-offs relates to the money available to the local climbing community. In the UK, there is a bolt fund that helps local bolters put up routes with good-quality lower-offs. However, where the climbing community is small and relatively poor, the lower-offs

SPORT CLIMBING

will be the cheapest available (even homemade) and may be in desperate need of replacing. It is also important to note that in very popular areas, some lower-offs can be so well used that the rings wear extremely thin.

Wherever you are, it is important to judge each lower-off as you find it and, if necessary, leave behind some of your own kit in order to be safe. I always carry an old snap-link as a bail-biner. This spare carabiner can be clipped to the lower-off bolts, if you don't like the ring or chain. You could also leave it on the penultimate bolt to backup a lower-off you do not completely trust. Most lower-offs are safe enough, but it is better to leave a bit of kit behind than risk injury or worse.

Threading the Lower-Off
There are a few different ways of threading the lower-off. Some are more efficient than others and some are safer than others. The method described below uses a cow's tail, and is the safest and simplest method and will work 99 per cent of the time.

I suppose the simplest possible method is just to attach yourself with a cow's tail, untie, thread the lower-off and tie back in. I had a friend who used to do this and it worked fine for a few years, until one day he dropped the rope. He had to wait, hanging in his harness in the dark for four hours, for his mate to go back to the car, drive to find help and come back to rescue him. He now uses the method below.

Clip the Rope As soon as you arrive at the lower-off, clip the rope to the lower-off using a quickdraw. Clip one of the bolts directly (or high on the chain in this case), leaving the ring of the lower-off free for the rope.

Cow's Tail In Clip your cow's tail into the other bolt (the one without a quickdraw in it) and do up the carabiner. You are now attached by two points (the rope to your belayer and your cow's tail) and are free to let go with your hands.

Pull Up Slack Bring up some slack from in front of your quickdraw (the rope between your knot and the quickdraw). The loop of slack needs to run from your knot, down to your feet and backup to your hands.

A double glue-in bolt lower-off.

Clip the rope.

SPORT CLIMBING

Cow's tail in.

Pull up slack.

Overhand Tie an overhand knot in the slack rope just in front of the quickdraw. You will need enough slack, from the overhand knot to your figure-of-eight, to thread the belay comfortably. Clip the overhand knot to your belay loop using a screw-gate carabiner and do it up.

Thread the Lower-Off Now you are backed up from the belayer to your overhand knot, you can untie your original figure-of-eight. This leaves the end of the rope free to be threaded through the lower-off, making sure you are threading rounded metal, and not a square-cut bolt or tat. Then tie back in as normal.

Dismantle, Check and Lower Now you can untie the overhand knot, remove the quickdraw and the belayer can take up all the slack. Make one final check that your rope is attached to your harness correctly and that the rope runs from your harness, through a rounded metal part of the lower-off and down to your belayer. Once you are sure that all is correct, remove your cow's tail to allow your belayer to lower you back down your route.

> **LOWER-OFFS: IN SHORT**
> - Always have two attachment points.
> - Make sure the rope runs over smooth, rounded metal.
> - Check everything before removing your cow's tail.
> - Judge each lower-off individually.
> - If in doubt, back it up.

58 SPORT CLIMBING

Overhand 1.

Overhand 2.

Overhand 3.

Overhand 4

Thread the lower-off 1.

SPORT CLIMBING 59

Thread the lower-off 2.

Dismantle, check and lower.

Dangers

There are four basic dangers to watch out for when lead climbing (they apply to trad as well). These dangers are back clipping, Z-clipping, having your leg behind the rope and the first third of your route.

Back Clipping

As described above, there is a right and wrong way to clip your rope to a quickdraw. The correct way is with the live rope coming out of the quickdraw, away from the rock and towards the climber. The wrong way is for the live rope to go through the front of the quickdraw, towards the rock, and running across the gate to the climber — this is called a back clip. In the event of a fall, a back-clipped quickdraw can unclip itself, which obviously compromises safety.

DANGER, this quickdraw is back-clipped.

DANGER, as climber falls, the rope comes away from the wall.

60 SPORT CLIMBING

DANGER, the rope folds over and opens the gate.

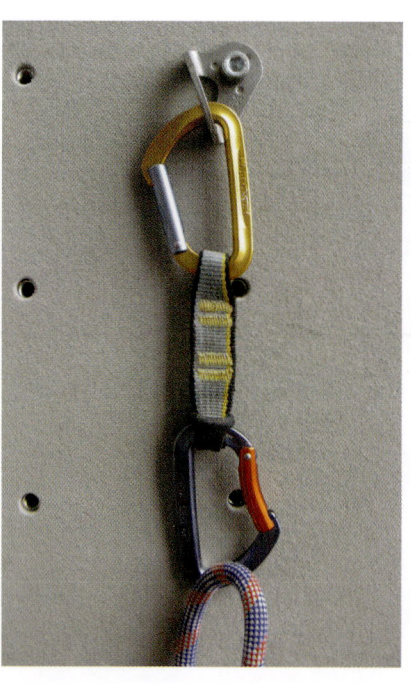

DANGER, the rope unclips from the snap link.

GOOD, this quickdraw is clipped correctly.

GOOD, as climber falls, the rope comes away from the wall.

GOOD, the rope falls clear of the gate.

GOOD, the rope is held in the snap link.

SPORT CLIMBING 61

GOOD, legs are clear of the rope.

SPORT CLIMBING

Z-Clipping
The bolts on a route should be clipped in turn. Z-clipping occurs when you reach down too far and clip the rope below your last quickdraw into a quickdraw above your head. This creates a Z in the rope, as you have essentially clipped the second quickdraw first and the first one second. The problem is that now you will have too much friction in the system to carry on climbing. Also, if you are low down the route, you could be in danger, as you have essentially missed out a bolt.

Leg Behind the Rope
You can think about the wall, the rope and your legs as a sandwich. You always want the rope as the filling. If your leg gets between the rope and the wall, then a fall could be very dangerous, burning your skin and flipping you upside down.

BAD, this rope has been Z-clipped.

DANGER, rope behind the leg.

SPORT CLIMBING

ABOVE: GOOD, if the foot slipped, there is little chance of it catching behind the rope.

TOP RIGHT: BAD, keeping rope over your thigh sometimes leaves the chance of your foot catching the rope.

BOTTOM RIGHT: DANGER, if the foot slipped, the rope would definitely catch the leg.

Potentially, you could be flipped over, hard enough for you to hit the back of your head against the rock with your body upside down – to be avoided.

Below you will see a few examples of good, bad and dangerous positions for the rope to be in relation to your leg while climbing. It is impossible to demonstrate every possible position for every given move. Try to visualize what the result of a fall would be and avoid positions where the rope could catch your leg if you fell off.

SPORT CLIMBING

The First Third

The worst-case scenario of any fall is hitting the ground. The further away from the ground you climb, the safer you get. However, if you come to a massive ledge on your route, then this ledge should be treated in the same way you would treat the ground under your belayer's feet.

As a belayer and a climber, there is plenty to think about for the first few clips. Listed below are some issues to be aware of, which should help keep the climber safe.

Belayer: Where to Stand? When a climber falls off, the rope from the belayer to the first clip will become ridged and straight, like an iron bar. Standing directly behind the climber for the first few clips, therefore, is like holding an iron bar behind them... not very helpful. It is best to stand to one side, leaving a clear fall zone for the climber.

Belayer: Slack or Tight? Obviously the climber needs some slack in order to move, and clip. If the rope is too tight, you could even pull them off the route as they are about to clip, which would not put you in their good books. However, the climber at the bottom of their route only has a small space between them and the floor to fall into, so too much slack will render the belayer useless. A fine balance needs to be struck between too slack and too tight.

Belayer: What If They Fall at the Wrong Time? If your climber falls at the wrong moment, no matter what you do, they may hit the floor. This is particularly true of routes with hard second clips where the climber may be reaching high to clip at the moment they fall off. A quick-reacting belayer might be able to take in some slack (with their arms or by running backwards) while the climber is in the air, thus stopping them hitting the

BAD, belayer behind the climber 1.

BAD, belayer behind the climber 2.

SPORT CLIMBING 65

GOOD, belayer to the side of the climber 1.

GOOD, belayer to the side of the climber 2.

floor. But be aware that this will slam the climber (to be discussed further below), which could be just as damaging as hitting the ground. The judgment is the belayer's to make.

Climber: When to Clip? It is often the case that you will clip as soon as you possibly can. Sometimes, however, this can put you in a stressful clipping position, which can take away valuable energy for the rest of the route. Clipping way above your head is also potentially more dangerous than clipping at a comfortable height, as you need to pull out more slack to clip with than you would to climb up to the bolt. As a result, if you fall while trying to clip, you will fall further than if you climbed up to the bolt and clipped from there. A common mistake is desperately trying to clip a quickdraw way above your head, off some horrendously poor hold, when you could make one more move up and clip comfortably from a massive hold next to the quickdraw. It is best to clip from comfortable positions, not necessarily as soon as you can.

CLIMBER DANGERS: IN SHORT

- Avoid back clipping.
- Avoid z-clipping.
- Keep your legs outside the rope.
- Clip from comfortable positions.

BELAYER DANGER: IN SHORT

- The first third is the danger zone.
- Stand to one side.
- Keep the rope slack enough so that the climber can move.
- Keep the rope close enough to keep the climber safe.

BAD, clipping from a poor hold far below the quickdraw puts a lot of extra slack in the system and is very strenuous.

GOOD, clipping when next to the quickdraw from a good hold puts no extra slack in the system and is far less strenuous.

Falling

Falling off is part of climbing. Fear of falling is the biggest limitation you can put on your climbing ability. Understanding when it is safe to fall off, and how to react as a belayer, can turn falling from a scary experience to be avoided, into an enjoyable part of climbing.

How to Fall

As a climber, the only control you have over the quality of your belay is to choose your climbing partners carefully. However, you can protect yourself by falling in the right position. Keep your arms up when you fall. Have your legs ready to take any impact from hitting the wall. Avoid holding the rope, as it could give you a nasty friction burn or worse. Stay loose in the air – you are less prone to injury if you are relaxed.

Where Does the Force Go?

When top roping, the belayer's actions are either safe or unsafe. When lead belaying, however, there are many subtle levels between a good and a bad belayer. The physics of where the energy goes during a lead fall is complicated. I do not have a degree in physics (more's the pity), and therefore the following explanations come from experience of teaching and climbing, rather than mathematics and study. I will avoid technical jargon and explain the ideas in basic terms.

When your climber is falling through the air, there is potential energy. This is an amount of force that has to go somewhere. The belayer has four options as to where that force goes: the rope, the belay device, the belayer's body or the climber's body.

- **The rope.** Ropes stretch by approximately 10 per cent of their length, and this stretch absorbs a certain amount of force. If there is 10m of rope between the climber and the belayer, and the climber falls off, the rope will stretch by about 1m, softening the fall. It takes about ten minutes for the rope to return to its original length. This means that the first fall will feel soft, but one taken soon after will feel a lot harder.
- **The belay device.** If the belayer can allow, under tension, about 30cm of rope to slide through the belay device, just at the point that the weight of the climber comes onto the live rope, then the force is transformed into heat in the belay device. This takes a little skill and timing to get right but makes the climber's fall much softer and they only fall an additional 30cm. This technique does not work with assisted-braking devices such as the GRIGRI.
- **The belayer.** As the belayer takes the weight of the climber, they are likely to be pulled forward or even lifted off the ground. This is a very natural and efficient method of absorbing the force of a falling climber. The only trouble comes when a belayer is caught off-guard and trips or hits the wall hard. This technique does not work when using a ground anchor.
- **The climber.** If the other three systems for absorbing force are not used then it will all go through the climber's body. This will mean that they swing into the wall with great force and they dissipate the energy by bending their arms and legs as they make contact. This may work but can easily result in injury.

All four of these shock absorbers will come into play with every fall a climber takes. It is up to the belayer to choose how much force they distribute to each one. The exact levels will obviously change every time. If the climber takes the majority of the force through their body,

Chinano taking a very safe fall in Rodellar, Spain. © STEVE GORTON

we call this being slammed. If the climber takes very minimal force, and it is all taken up by the belayer and their device, then we call this a dynamic belay. Anything in the middle I will call a static belay, as will be described below.

How to Slam Your Climber

As the climber falls through the air, the belayer decides to take in as much slack as possible. They can do this by taking-in as normal, or by running backwards. This means that the climber will fall a shorter distance but will be slammed into the wall. In some circumstances this could be a good thing. In general, I would rather be slammed than to hit the floor or a ledge with any speed. Slamming your climber, however, can lead to injury and should therefore be avoided unless there is a danger of the climber hitting the floor or a ledge.

LEFT: *Slamming: climber falls off, the belayer starts to take in.*

BELOW LEFT: *Slamming: climber is in the air, the belayer steps back.*

BELOW RIGHT: *Slamming: climber's weight comes onto the rope, the belayer puts full force through the climber.*

SPORT CLIMBING

How to Give a Static Belay

A static belay is where you basically do nothing. You do not allow yourself to be pulled forward (because you are heavier than the climber or are ground-anchored), or let any rope through the belay device. The fact that the rope is stretchy will take up a lot of the force. However, if your climber falls off again within a few minutes, the rope will not stretch anywhere near as much and you will end up slamming them. If you are heavier than your climber, be aware that just standing still could put a lot of force through them.

RIGHT: Static: climber falls off, the belayer does not move.

BELOW LEFT: Static: climber is in the air, the belayer braces for impact.

BELOW RIGHT: Static: climber's weight comes onto the rope, the belayer resists the pull and stays in position.

How to Give a Dynamic Belay

In a dynamic belay we want virtually none of the force of the fall to be transferred to the climber. There is a small window of opportunity for the belayer to make this happen. The opportunity starts when the climber's weight hits the belay device and finishes when they come to a stop.

Using Your Body The easiest way to cushion the fall is with your body. As the weight of the climber hits your belay device, it will start to pull you forward, or up, towards the first quickdraw. Simply allow this to happen. Do not be tempted to start moving too early. If you see your mate in the air and immediately start running forward, then they will just fall this extra distance (creating more force) before the weight hits the belay device.

Using the Belay Device If you are belaying with a tubular device, it is possible to use it to give a dynamic belay to your climber. As the climber falls through the air, you do nothing (hopefully you are in the default start/stop position discussed above in giving slack with tubular devices). As the weight of the climber comes on to the belay device, bring your hand (still holding onto the dead rope) slowly forward to your hip between your waist and leg loops. It is like giving slack but in slow motion.

After giving this type of dynamic belay, you will notice that the belay device has become much warmer. This is where the force of the falling climber has gone. This method is obviously not possible with assisted-braking devices, but is pretty much the only way of giving a dynamic belay when ground-anchored.

Dynamic using your body: climber falls off, the belayer does not move.

Dynamic using your body: climber is in the air, the belayer prepares to be pulled forward and up.

Dynamic using your body: climber's weight comes onto the rope, the belayer allows themselves to be pulled forward and up.

SPORT CLIMBING

DYNAMIC BELAYING: IN SHORT

- The force of a fall can go into the rope, the belay device, the belayer or the climber.
- Only slam your climber if they are about to hit the floor or a ledge.
- You can give a dynamic belay using your body.
- You can give a dynamic belay using your belay device.

Fall Practice

Yes that's right! As a climber and a belayer it is important to become comfortable with falling when it is safe to do so. The best method I know of is the clip drop method.

Clip Drop

Choose a route that has minimal objective danger (relatively steep and with no large ledges). You decide what you are going to do and tell your belayer. On this occasion, after clipping the 6th, 7th and 8th clip, you will fall off straight away. Your belayer is now clear what is going to happen and, having chosen places to fall off that are a long way from the floor, you have given them a

Dynamic using the belay device: climber falls off, the belayer does not move.

Dynamic using the belay device: climber is in the air, the belayer prepares to bring the rope forward under tension.

Dynamic using the belay device: climber's weight comes onto the rope, the belayer allows the rope to be pulled slowly through the belay device until their hand is on their hip.

SPORT CLIMBING

> **FALLING: IN SHORT**
>
> - When you fall, be loose and relaxed in the air.
> - Try to fall every time you go climbing.
> - Practice turns fear into confidence.

chance to practise dynamic belaying. After completing the exercise, you discuss how it all felt. Was the belay dynamic enough or too dynamic? How scared were you, as the climber? Could you do something a little more adventurous next time?

The clip drop method is great because it works for all abilities. Try starting out by clipping a quickdraw way above your head, counting to three and jumping off. To progress from this, you could fall off as soon as the rope is clipped in. From there you can work yourself higher and higher above your quickdraw, always staying within your comfort zone until falling is an experience to enjoy.

We all need to keep reminding ourselves that falling is OK. So long as the objective dangers are avoided, and you have a good belayer, there is no reason to be scared. But the mind needs physically reminding of this on a regular basis. Make falling part of your routine and you will become a better, more confident climber.

Ground Anchors for Sport Climbing

When a lead belayer needs a ground anchor, it is best to use the rope. As described before, the rope is stretchy so will help the belayer to give a more dynamic belay. In addition to this, the knots will tighten up, absorbing force as they pull in around themselves.

When indoors, there will be a ground anchor or ballast bag. Outdoors, you will need to look for a tree, a tree root or a boulder to attach to. Start by threading a sling around your ground anchor and tying-in to the bottom end of the rope pile. Clip the rope (around a metre from your knot) to the sling using a carabiner and a clove hitch (see Chapter 10 for how to tie a clove hitch). If there is nothing else available, you could use your rucksack filled with your kit and a few rocks as a ballast bag. As with all ground-anchor methods, make sure you are standing in front of the anchor so that ABC is in line (as with a top-rope ground anchor), that you are held tightly in position and that your arms are free to move and belay effectively.

> **JARGON**
>
> **Bail-biner:** a spare carabiner carried specifically to leave behind in an emergency.
> **In situ:** anything that is already in place and does not need to be placed by the climber.
> **Lower-off:** two bolts liked together that can be threaded in order to be lower back to the ground.
> **Mallion:** an oval carabiner with a barrel-threaded opening.
> **Racking up:** arranging all your equipment on your harness.
> **Tat:** generic term for old cut-off of rope or sling.
> **Webbing:** a length of strong nylon that does not stretch.
> **Working routes:** working out a route in sections with a view to climbing it cleanly at a later stage (also called redpointing).

Ground anchor, using the rope.

> **GROUND ANCHORS: IN SHORT**
>
> - Use the rope when lead belaying.
> - Use your rucksack if there is nothing else available.
> - Anchor, Belayer and Climber (ABC) in line.
> - Make sure you are held in position.
> - Be sure your arms are free to belay.

CHAPTER 10

TRAD CLIMBING

Trad Climbing Kit List

Shoes

See Chapter 7 for climbing shoe details.

Chalk and Chalk Bag

See Chapter 7 for details of chalk and chalk bags.

Harness

See Chapter 8 for details of harnesses.

Belay Device and Screw-Gate Carabiner

See Chapter 8 for details on belay devices and screw gates.

Helmet

In Chapter 9 helmets are discussed in full. My advice is that you should always wear a helmet if your crag is large, slabby or loose. If you are not sure if you need to wear one or not, then it would be wise to wear one. Traditional climbs, particularly in the easier grades, tend to have more objective danger in terms of ledges and other protrusions you could hit as you fall, so it is recommended that a helmet is worn on all but the steepest lines.

Quickdraws

It is possible to use sport-climbing quickdraws for trad climbing but there are some advantages to having a separate set.

Robert Canavan climbing a bold traditional route in the Peak District. © STEVE GORTON

74 TRAD CLIMBING

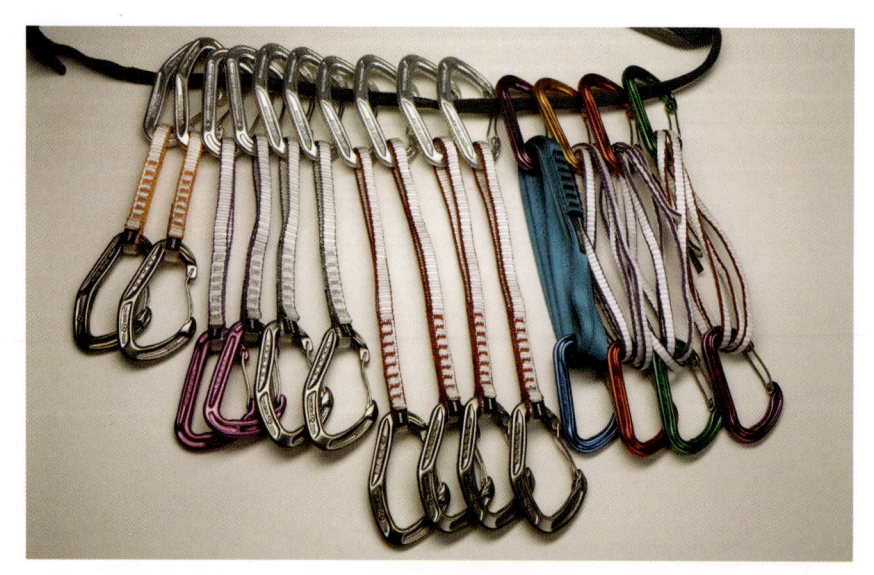

LEFT: Quickdraws for trad climbing.

BELOW: A set of wires.

through them. The wedge of metal is placed into a constriction in the rock and the wire is clipped with a quickdraw. They come in sizes ranging from a few millimetres to a few inches across, the sizes and number you buy will depend on where you intend to climb. Most climbing shops will sell a set of midrange wires that will suit most climbers. Be aware that extremely small wires are not very strong and require great judgment and experience before trusting them.

Trad climbers generally have a lot of equipment to carry up their route. Shaving off fifty grams per quickdraw could take half a kilo or more off the total load, which can make a huge difference over fifty metres of hard climbing. Super-thin quickdraws can be harder to handle and clip but the advantage of a light rack generally outweighs this disadvantage.

Trad routes can be much longer than sport routes (sometimes full rope lengths of 60m in one go). They also tend to wander up natural lines rather than follow a straight line of bolts. The rope running from one side of the cliff to the other, and back again can put a lot of friction into the system, making it harder to move as you get higher up your route. Using some long, or extendable, quickdraws can reduce this effect massively. See the section below on rope drag for a full description of extendible quickdraws and when to use them.

A good set of quickdraws for trad would be made up of two small, eight mid-length and four extendible quickdraws.

Wires

Wires (also called nuts) are wedges of metal of varying sizes with a wire running

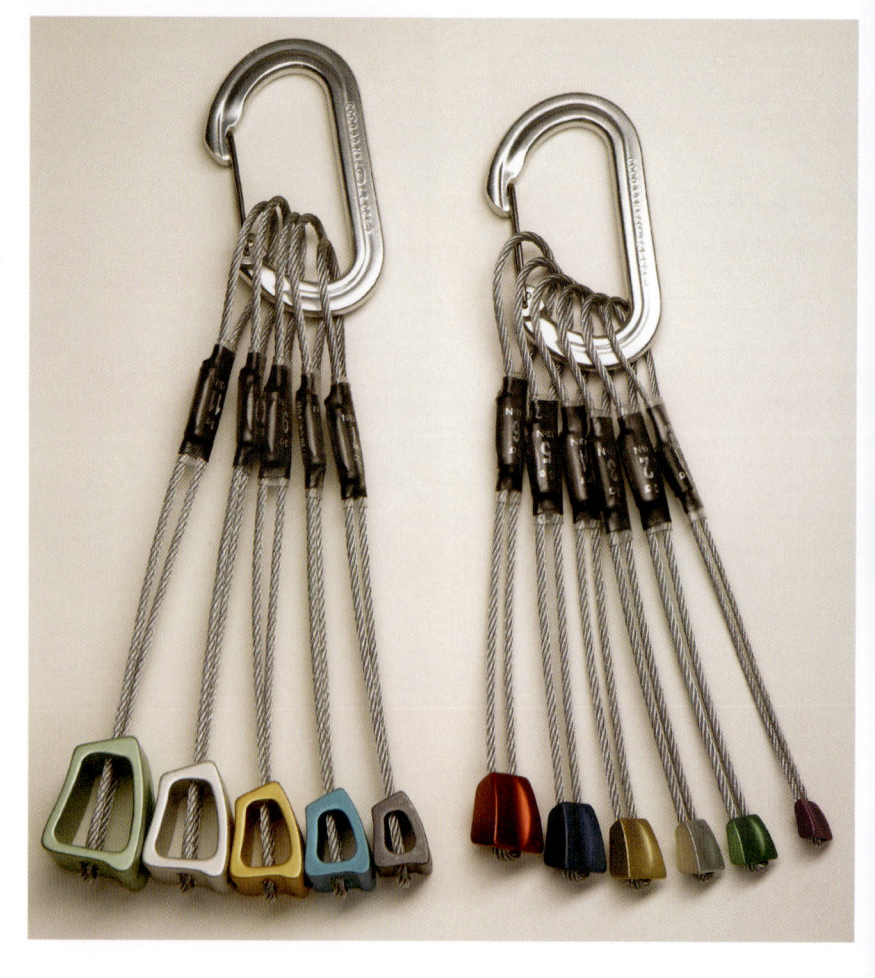

TRAD CLIMBING 75

ABOVE: A normal range of cams.

LEFT: Hexes.

Hexes

Hexes are very large wedges of metal with webbing instead of wire running through them. A few years ago they were a must for any trad climber, but are seen as a little old school these days, since the rise of cams. I will not say that they are essential but they can be very useful.

Cams

Cams are mechanical devices that get smaller when you depress the trigger and spring back when you let go. They are placed into cracks with parallel sides and their action means that the more weight applied, the more they press into the sides of the crack.

Cams revolutionized rock climbing in the 1980s and are now seen as a must-have piece of kit. They come in a variety of sizes to fit all cracks from a few millimetres across to massive one-foot wide monsters. The average trad climber needs about five cams; start with a cam as wide as your finger through to the size of your fist.

Nut Key

A nut key is used to help retrieve wires or cams that have wedged awkwardly into the rock.

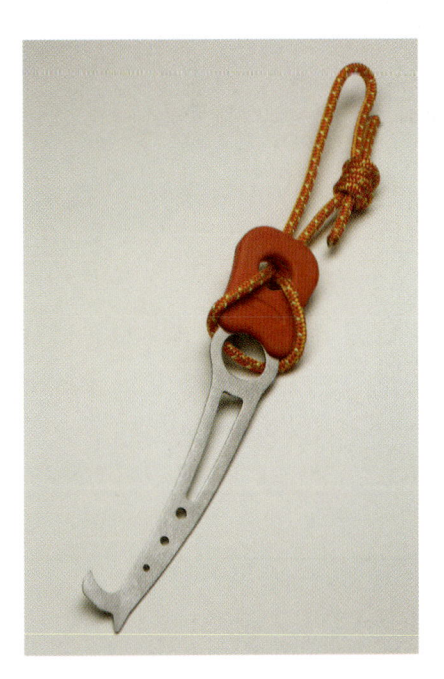

A nut key.

76 TRAD CLIMBING

Large, pear-shaped screw-gate carabiner.

Two small D-shaped carabiners.

Screw-Gate Carabiners

See Chapter 8 for details of carabiners. When anchoring yourself to the top of your route (or at a belay point), you will need a few screw gates. Generally it is good to have one large pear-shaped screw gate and a few small D-shaped ones.

Slings

Slings are loops of webbing. They are used

ABOVE: *Two 120cm slings with carabiners.*

LEFT: *Double ropes.*

TRAD CLIMBING

for a variety of jobs such as threading around trees or spikes for protection while climbing, for building belays and extending anchors. Pretty much all trad climbers will have a couple of slings on their harness or over their shoulder. They come in a variety of sizes and what you carry will depend on the style of rock you are climbing. A couple of 120cm slings are a good start.

Double Ropes

You can trad climb with a single rope but double ropes hold all the advantages. With double ropes you can reduce the rope drag mentioned earlier (and to be discussed in more detail later), and you can abseil twice as far. They take a little time to get used to but, ultimately, they are the better tool for trad climbing and a must for long multi-pitch routes. Double ropes are usually thinner than single ropes, between 8 and 9mm in diameter, so be sure your belay device is designed to be used with such thin ropes.

Prusiks

A prusik is a length of thin cord (5mm thick works well) that is tied together to make a loop. It is best to keep two on your harness, as will be explained in Chapter 13. Three metres of cord makes two good prusiks. Simply cut the length in half, seal the ends with a flame and tie the ends together with two opposing stopper

---

BUYING A TRAD RACK

- Shoes, chalk, harness, belay device, helmet.
- Two small, eight medium and four extendible quickdraws.
- Wires, at least one full midrange set.
- Cams, a range to fit finger to fist width cracks.
- Two 120cm slings.
- A nut key.
- Two prusiks (buy 3m of 5mm cord).
- Consider double ropes.
- Consider hexes.

Prusiks.

78 TRAD CLIMBING

LEFT: Well-racked harness for trad leading.

BELOW: The belayer has tied into both ropes and is flaking them out.

You climb up your route, placing protection as you see fit, clipping the rope to the protection with your quickdraws. Once you arrive at the top, you attach yourself to something solid (boulders, trees or gear placed in the rock), pull in all the excess slack and put your mate on belay. They then climb the route on top rope (often called seconding), removing your gear from the route as they go. Arriving at the top they have left the route completely clear of your kit.

A couple of back slaps later, you walk back down to the bottom and chose a route for your partner to lead.

Prep: Trad Climbing

The climber will rack up, which means they get all the equipment they will need for the route on to their harness, in a neat, orderly fashion. Generally, the things you will need when climbing, such as quickdraws and wires, will go on the front gear loops and the equipment for building belays will go at the back. Your chalk bag should be on a piece of string and sit neatly at the back of your harness.

knots (known as a fisherman's knot). They are used to grip the rope by wrapping them around it, creating friction. There are mechanical devices on the market that do the same thing but they tend to be one-directional and not so easy to remove under load. The Shunt works well as a mechanical alternative but is massively heavy by comparison.

How It All Works

You and your friend pack up your kit, along with lunch, and head to the crag. After finding your route, you unpack the kit and flake out the rope. As you have decided to climb first, you rack up (arrange all the necessary kit on your harness) and tie into the top end of the rope. Your belayer will also tie-in but to the bottom end of the rope pile and put you on belay a couple of metres from your knot.

The belayer will flake out the rope, piling it up onto itself. As they do this, they will be checking for abrasions, unwanted knots and that the rope will lift off the top of the rope pile smoothly. If you are using double ropes, flake each rope out separately.

The belayer should tie-in to the bottom end of the rope and belay from their rope loop, rather than their belay loop. The rope loop stretches under load and therefore absorbs some of the energy during a fall, plus it gives you one less job to do later, as you will eventually be climbing the route on top rope anyway.

Check Each Other Before Climbing: Trad Climbing

It is vital that you get into the habit of checking your partner before you start climbing. It's something like the buddy system in diving. Even the most experienced climbers in the world can make mistakes.

As a belayer you must check your climber:

- Waist belt – is it tight enough and doubled back, if necessary?
- Attachment points – is the knot attached to tie-in loops?
- Knot(s) – is it rethreaded correctly?

As a climber you must check your belayer:

- Waist belt – is it tight enough and doubled back, if necessary?
- Attachment point – is the belay device attached to the rope loop?
- Screw gate – is it done up?
- Knot(s) – is the belayer tied into the bottom end of the rope(s) correctly?

These checks ensure the basic safety chain is in place and will take approximately ten seconds each time. Get into the habit as soon as you can, this is not just a safety precaution but also gives you confidence when pulling hard moves further up your route.

Trad Lead Belaying

Technically, there is not much difference between sport and trad belaying. When trad belaying, however, it is important that you stay close to the wall. Bolts can take a pull from any direction, whereas wires (and cams depending on the placement) can only take a downward force. If a belayer is standing far away from the wall when the climber falls off, the first piece of protection is pulled up and away from the wall; this can lift out the first piece of gear. In fact, there are stories of the entire pitch being stripped in this way, leaving

Double rope paying out: the top hand pulls only the red rope through the device. The bottom hand's little finger splits the ropes.

Double rope paying out: the top hand holds both ropes above the device.

Double rope paying out: the bottom hand slides down both ropes.

Double rope taking in: the bottom hand pinches the red rope with the blue rope still running through the same hand.

Double rope taking in: as the red rope is taken in the blue rope runs through the same hand.

Double rope taking in: both ropes are locked off as normal.

TRAD CLIMBING

the climber hanging on a single wire forty metres off the deck. This danger can be removed by placing a multi-directional piece of gear at the start of the route, such as a thread (see sling section) but even so, it is generally worth getting in the habit of standing a little closer to the wall as a trad belayer.

Dynamic belaying was discussed at length in the last chapter, on sport climbing, and I will not spend too much time on it here. However, it is worth noting that the more force you can absorb with your body and the belay device, the less force is impacted into the gear the climber has placed. This is not a worry when the gear is solid number 10 wire, but if they are relying heavily on a marginal piece, then it could be the difference between it ripping out of the wall or staying put.

If belaying with double ropes, make sure you take the time to get each rope nicely piled up separately. It can be useful to keep your little finger between each rope so that they are separated before going into the belay device. A little practice can mean you can pay out and take in each rope separately without letting go of either rope at any time (see photos of this in practice). The belayer is paying out the red rope and then taking it back in without moving or letting go of the blue rope. This will take practice but eventually you will be belaying with double ropes as efficiently as with a single.

Trad Top-Rope Belaying

When trad climbing you will find that you have to be able to belay from any direction. When you get to the top of a climb, you will have to belay from above your climber. When multi-pitching, you may have to belay someone sideways as they head out onto their pitch, with your left or right hand on the dead rope, depending on the climber's route and not your personal preference.

The golden rule here is that the dead rope must be on the opposite side to the climber, so that you lock off away from them. Locking off downwards when you are above the climber will leave the belay device in an unlocked position. At the top of your route then, you take in by 'upside down V' to the shoulder, one, two, three.

This method is exactly the same as the taking in method discussed in Chapter 8, but upside down. Whatever the position of the climber, relative to you, be sure to lock off away from them.

Start/Stop Point This is your default position when belaying from the top. With the dead rope locked off away from the climber.

Upside-Down V Bring the dead rope down towards the climber, taking live rope through the device.

To the Shoulder Lock the device backup towards your shoulder.

Start/stop point, locked off away from the climber.

TOP LEFT: *Upside down V.*

TOP RIGHT: *To the shoulder.*

BOTTOM LEFT: *One.*

One Bring the hand on the live rope up to the dead rope near the device.

Two Bring the top hand down to meet the bottom hand (back into its original position).

Three Bring the bottom hand down to the live rope ready to take in again.

Placing Traditional Gear

There are many different options for placing gear when trad climbing. You are, of course, bound by what the rock has to offer. A blank face of rock may have no options whatsoever, whereas a route that follows a crack system may have more gear than you can shake a quickdraw at.

Generally, so long as you have not chosen a massively run-out route (see Chapter 3), then there will be something worth placing when you need it. There are many tricks used in trad climbing. People do things like stack wires together if they do not

TRAD CLIMBING

Two.

Three.

have the right size, or link wires together to reach for far away placements. If you trad climb with a few different partners, you will pick up tricks that will help from time to time, but for now I will stick to the basics. We will go through wire, cam and sling placements. There is more gear out there, in less common use, but if you have a good basis in wires, cams and slings, then you should be able to work out (having read the instructions) how to use more obscure gear, safely.

Score Your Gear Out of 10

Whatever gear you place, get into the habit of scoring it out of 10. If you place a piece that is so poor you would not want to hang your car keys from it, then it gets 1/10. If you place a piece that you would happily hang your car from, then it gets 10/10. Simple.

Getting into this habit helps you make quick judgments about your gear as you move up the rock. Unfortunately you cannot always have 10/10 gear. But on an easier section of the route, you may decide that 5/10 is enough, whereas just below a hard crux, you definitely want 10/10, or two pieces, say one 7/10 and one 8/10.

How you judge this gear will be discussed below. But really, the more experience you get placing gear, the better you will get at judging how likely it is to hold you if you fall off. Get out climbing easy routes, getting as much gear in as possible and you will find your average score going up.

Wires

Wires are placed on their side the majority of the time. However, by turning them straight on they will fit slightly larger cracks, which can be very useful when you are running low. A good wire placement requires a constriction in the rock, ideally a crack that gets thinner at the bottom and has a slight thinning at the front of the crack too. A well-placed wire should look like it was born to fit into the crack, the more metal touching rock the better.

The diagrams are of perfect wire placements. All four corners of the metal wedge are touching the rock, and two sides of the wedge are in complete contact with the sides of the crack. The crack itself has solid rock on either side and gets thinner below the wire, so that

84 TRAD CLIMBING

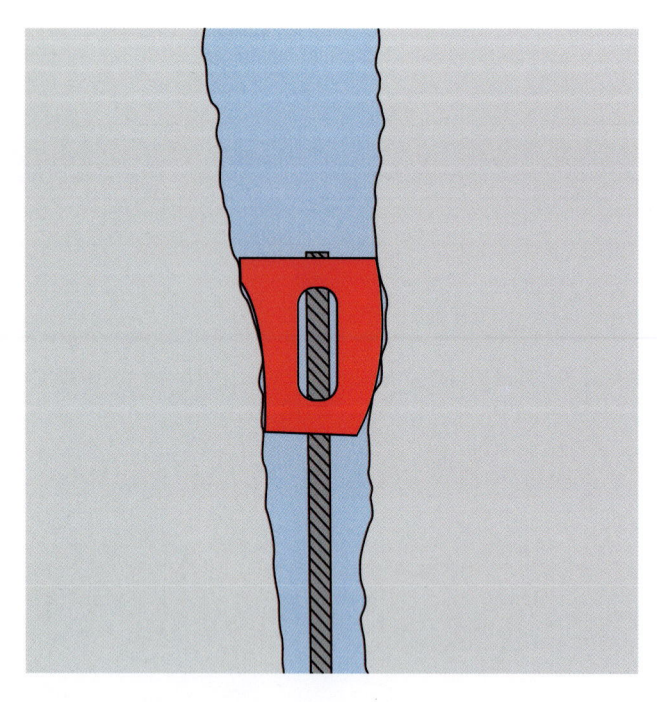

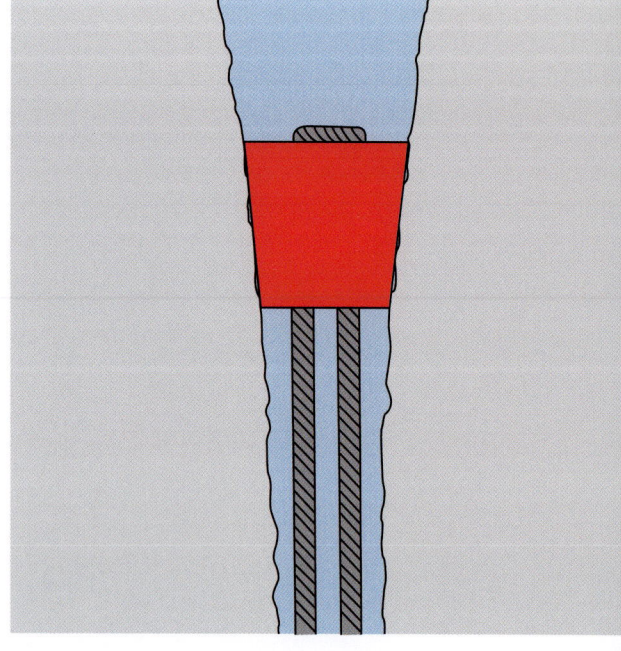

GOOD, wire placed on its side.

GOOD, wire placed straight on.

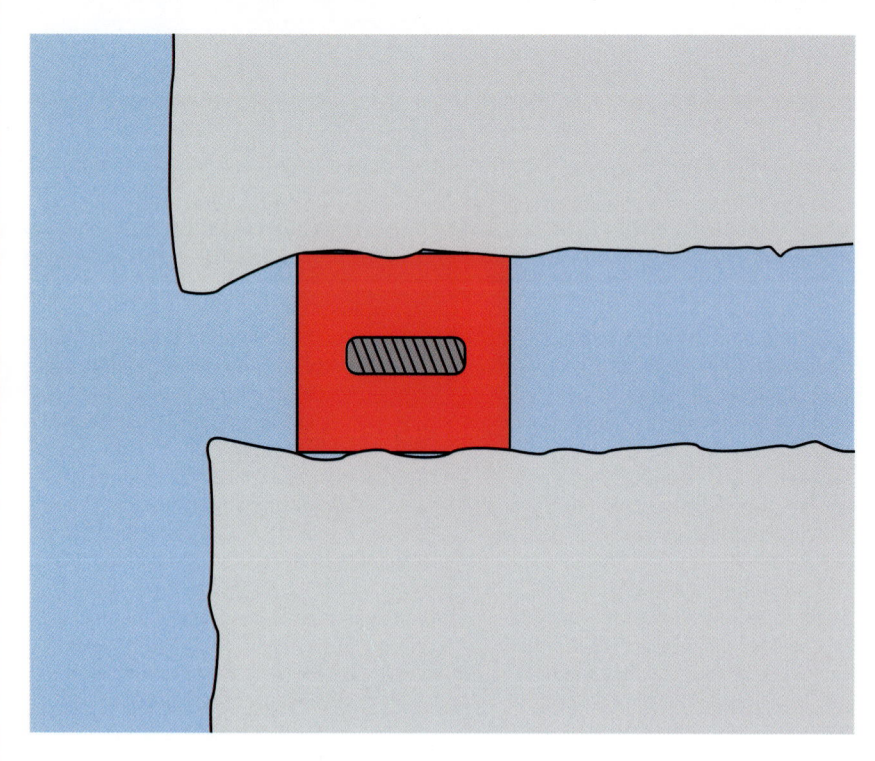

GOOD, wire placement viewed from above.

even if the rock around the wedge should crumble a little, the wire will just fall into a tighter gap. These placements are my 10/10 for wires.

Choosing the wrong part of the crack, or wire for that crack, can easily make your placements virtually useless. Cracks that flare outwards towards you do not offer good options for gear, particularly when using wires. You may be able to get the back-half of the wire to stick in place, but a fall is likely to pull it out. Equally, cracks that become significantly wider inside can have the same problem. The front half of the wire may stick but any movement could knock it back into the space behind. If your wire is not completely touching rock on all corners, then treat it with caution.

It is also important to remember that your gear is only as good as the rock around it. If the rock you place your gear behind is thin, and/or sounds hollow when you tap it, then the rock could easily break away when you weight it.

TRAD CLIMBING

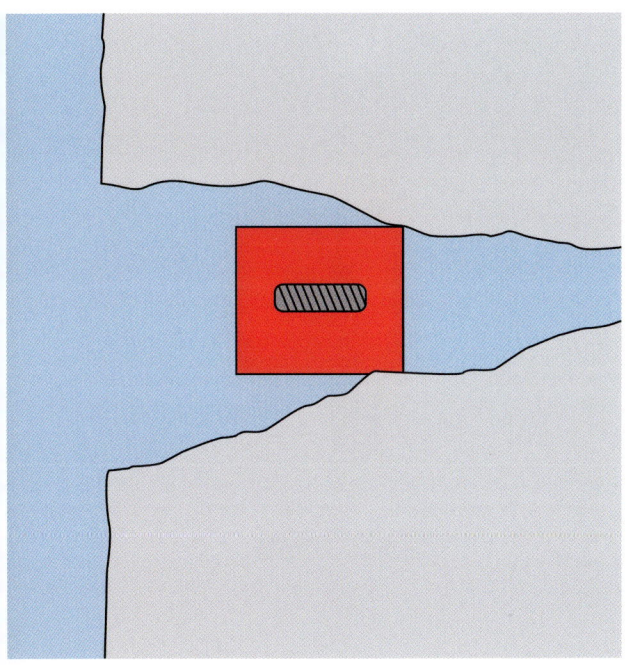

DANGER, wire placed in a flaring crack.

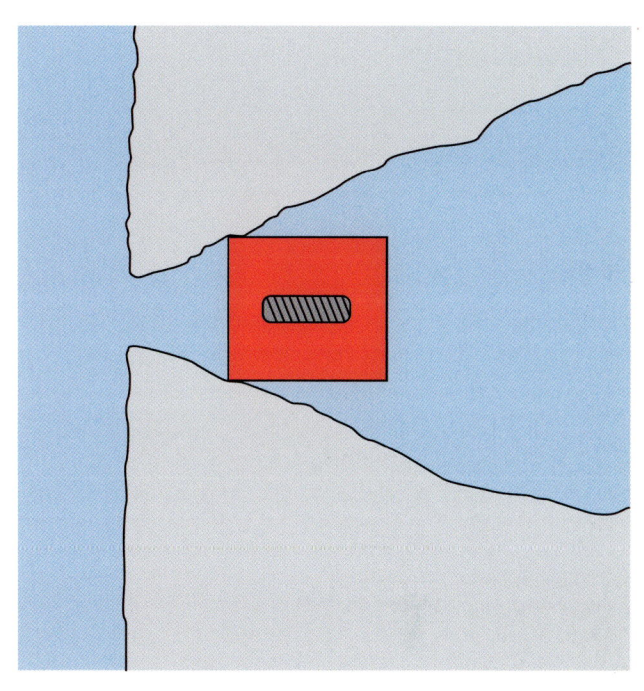

DANGER, wire placed in a concave crack.

DANGER, wire placed behind thin (weak) rock.

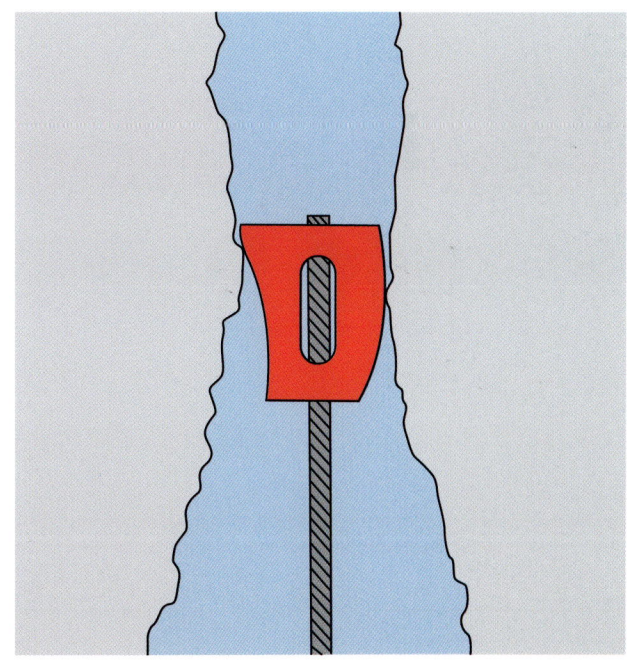

DANGER, wire relies on a small (weak) area of rock.

86 TRAD CLIMBING

> **WIRES: IN SHORT**
> - Look for a constriction in the crack.
> - All four corners should be touching the rock.
> - Your gear is only as good as the rock around it.

Cams

Cams are designed to be placed in parallel-sided cracks. There are a few important things to remember when placing a cam.

Arms
Make sure all the cam's 'arms' are in contact with the rock and that both sides are pretty much equal in angle. All four arms must be loaded equally, otherwise the cam is likely to twist and, ultimately, fall out.

Camming Angle
If the arms of your cam are only just pulled in, then your cam will have a small camming angle. This will result in the cam being very unstable and completely reliant on the millimetre or so of rock touching the edges of the arms. If the tiny fragment of rock, touching the arms of your cam, crumbles under your weight, then the cam will start to move and potentially come out of the crack completely.

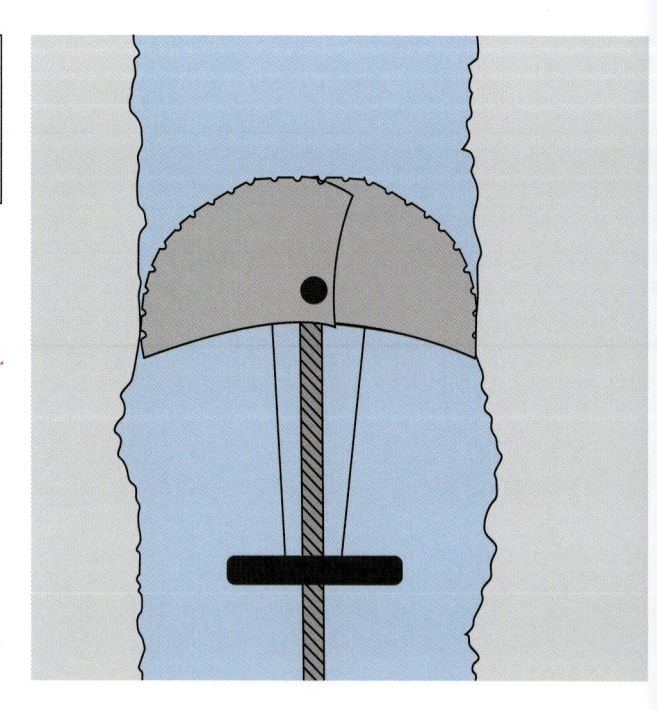

DANGER, the arms are under-cammed and rely on a small area of rock.

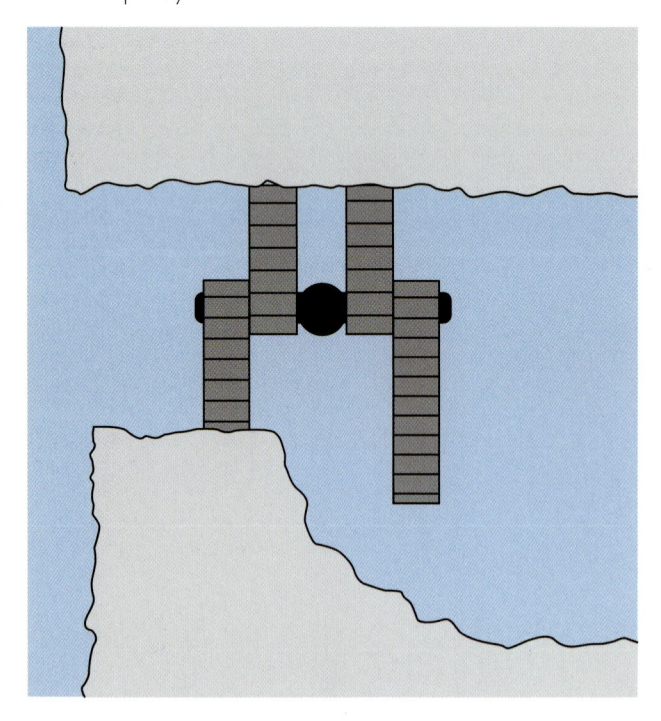

DANGER, one arm not touching the rock.

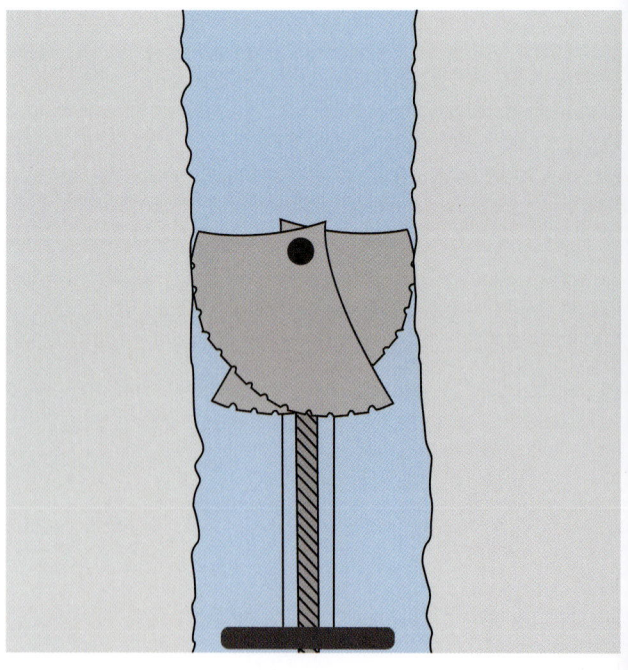

BAD, the arms are over-cammed, it will not bite well and will be hard to remove.

TRAD CLIMBING 87

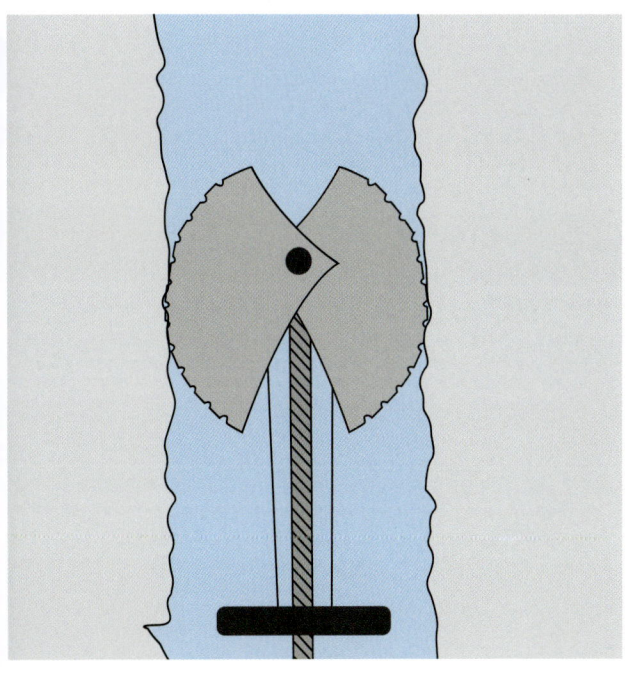

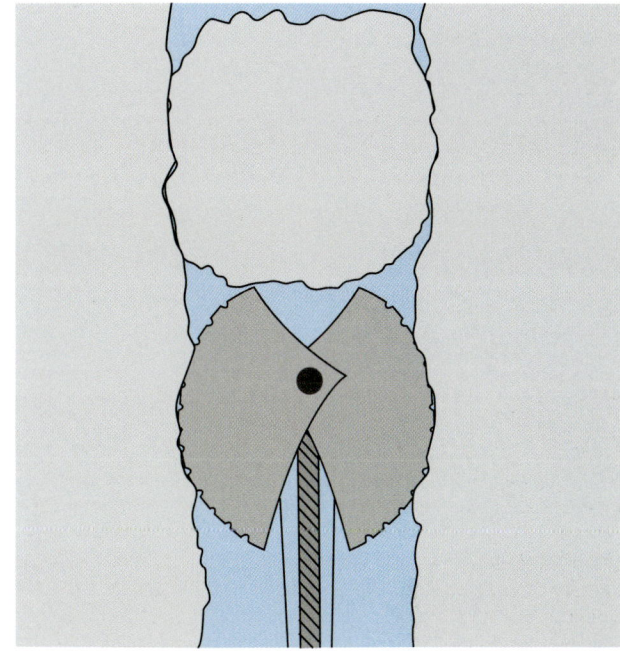

GOOD, arms cammed in the mid range.

GOOD, arms cammed in the mid range and blocked to prevent the cam walking.

If the arms are pulled in too much (over-cammed), then the cam finds it difficult to initiate the outward push required to hold your weight. This is worrying, as an over-cammed placement can look and feel solid but falling onto it would rip it straight out of the wall. The other problem with over-camming your expensive cam is that it makes them very hard to remove. You need to be able to make the cam smaller in order to remove it from the crack, so try not to ram them in too tightly or it may turn into a very expensive climbing trip.

The perfect camming angle is when the arms are pulled in halfway. This gives the most outward force in a fall, is the most stable of placements and will be easy for your partner to remove.

Walking

Just because your cam looked good when you placed it, doesn't mean it will still look like that when you are five metres above it. If you place a cam in a perfectly parallel crack and then start lifting and lowering the stem of the cam, it will happily start wandering off deeper and deeper into the crack. The problem is, first, that the cam could have walked into a poor placement and, second, it could have walked so far back that your partner cannot reach it to remove it from the rock. Unfortunately, as you climb above your cam the rope will gently lift the stem up and down initiating this walking tendency.

There are two methods of reducing the chance of your cam walking: extending

> **CAMS: IN SHORT**
> - All four arms touching rock and equally weighted.
> - Avoid over- or under-camming the arms; midway is the best camming angle.
> - Use obstacles in the crack or extendable quickdraws to ensure the cam doesn't walk.
> - Your gear is only as good as the rock around it.

the quickdraw or seating the cam where it cannot move.

Extending your quickdraw means that the rope will lift the sling of the quickdraw more than the stem of the cam. If you are taking a very sharp turn in your route, then this will only help a little but, in general, it will reduce the likelihood of your cam walking too far out of place.

Seating your cam where it cannot move is by far the best option. If you choose a point in the crack that has a natural bowl shape on either side, then the cam should stay put. Even better would be to place the cam with some sort of obstacle above the arms, such as a chock stone or a point where the crack suddenly gets thinner. This is the only sure-fire way of knowing that your cam will not move, once you climb past it.

Slings

Slings are often used at the belay stance, as discussed later, but are also very useful

TRAD CLIMBING

A sling threaded around a chock stone.

A sling draped over a spike.

on the route, as protection or for extending a particularly out-of-the-way piece of gear. As protection they are used for draping over spikes of rock or for threading natural features.

Draping
If you come across a spike of rock on your route that is solid, then you can simply drape your sling around it and clip it with a carabiner or quickdraw. The possible issue is that the sling could lift off the spike as you make your way further up the route. You can avoid this issue by making sure you have extended the sling well or, if you can spare the kit, you can leave a few pieces of gear hanging on the sling to weigh it down.

Threading
Let's imagine that your rock face has a tree root coming out of a crack and back into the crack. The root is as thick as your arm and strong. To make use of this fantastic piece of natural protection, simply pass your sling around the root and clip the two ends together. Sometimes these treads are made by natural rock features or from a rock that has become wedged in a crack (called a chock stone).

With chock stones, be careful not to load the gap where the chock stone meets the solid rock wall. If you fall off with your sling loading this gap, it will do its best to squeeze in between the chock stone and the wall, often damaging the sling and/or making it impossible to recover.

> **SLINGS: IN SHORT**
> - Extend or weight draped slings.
> - Thread natural features but avoid loading the gap.
> - Your sling is only as strong as the rock or tree you put it around.

TRAD CLIMBING

Avoiding Rope Drag

Every time your rope touches anything below you while you are leading a route, rubbing over rock or through your quickdraws, for example, it creates rope drag. The sharper the angle the rope takes around an object, the more friction (and therefore drag) is created. There are two solutions for reducing this drag effect. One is to use double ropes and the other is to extend your quickdraws. Outlined below are the basics for how to avoid rope drag. In the real world you will come across scenarios that will need careful thought, but these principles are a good start.

Rope Drag on Twin Cracks

Let's imagine you are climbing a route that goes straight up a vertical line of holds, with cracks running up either side of the holds. As you climb the route, you place gear in either crack alternately. Using a single rope and short quickdraws in this situation will create massive amounts of drag as the rope pulls through the quickdraws. Using a single rope, but extending the quickdraws, will reduce the drag significantly. Using double ropes and clipping one rope on the left crack and one on the right will massively reduce the rope drag to the point where it is negligible.

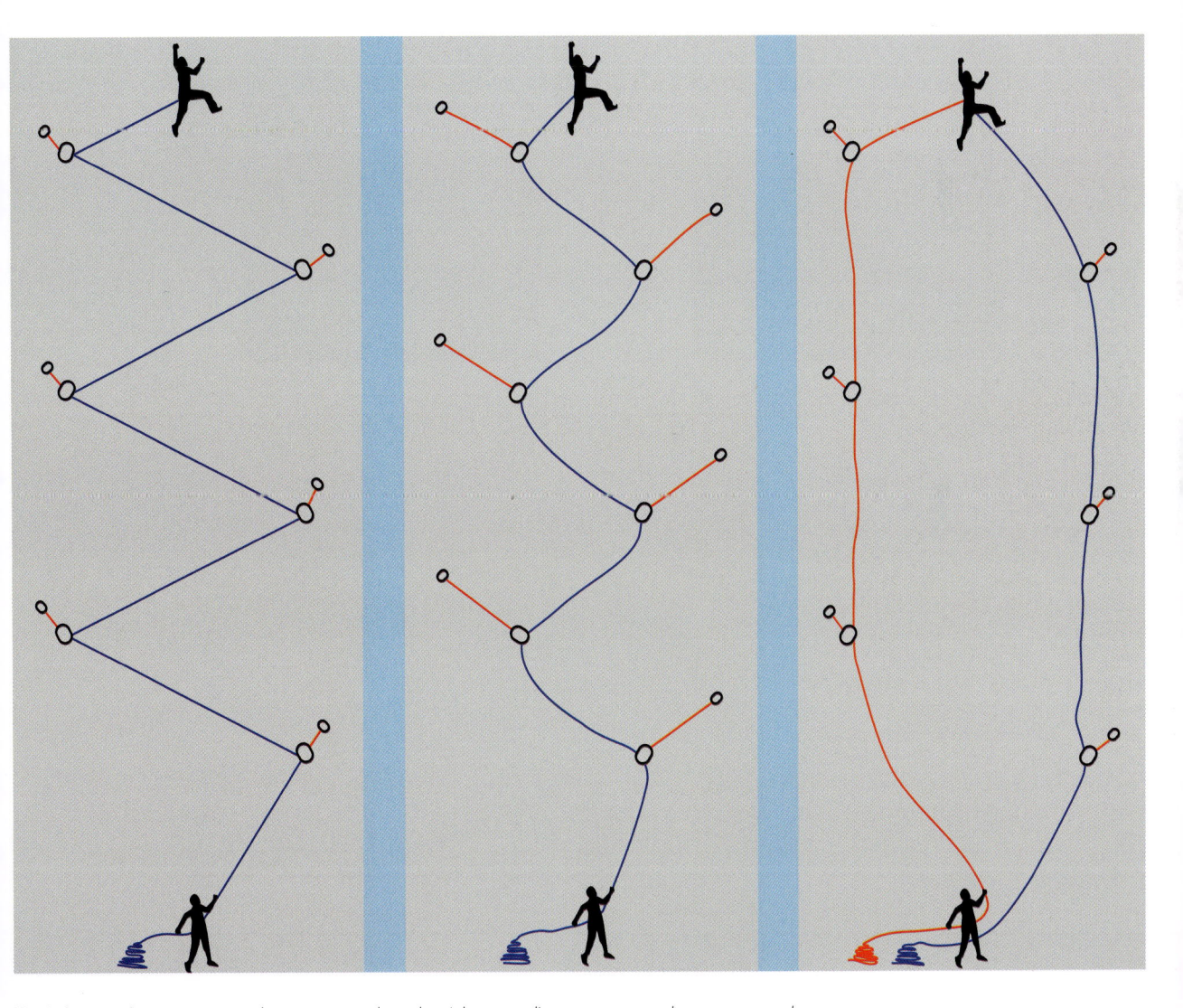

The left-most diagram creates the most rope drag, the right-most diagram creates almost no rope drag.

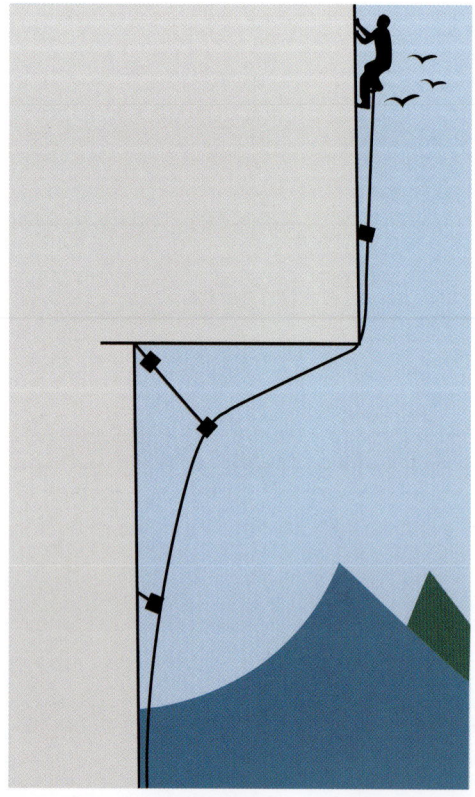

90 TRAD CLIMBING

Extending the quickdraws under the roof make for much less rope drag further up.

BOTTOM LEFT: One 60cm sling and two snap links.

BOTTOM RIGHT: Pass the bottom snap-link through the top one.

Rope Drag Through a Roof

Now let's imagine that you have come up to a steep overhang or small roof that has a crack at the base where you want to place some gear. A short quickdraw will be fine until you have turned the lip of the overhang. From then on the rope pulling over this edge can create huge amounts of friction, making climbing higher impossible. Extending this quickdraw will reduce the rope drag significantly. You will fall a little further should you come off the moves through the roof but, on the other hand, you will be able to carry on climbing once you have past the steep section.

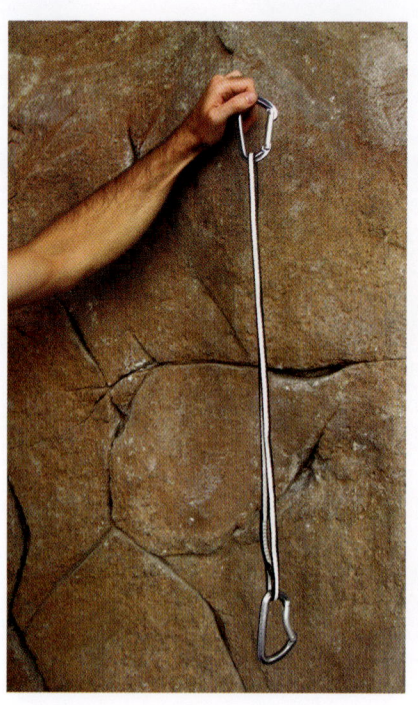

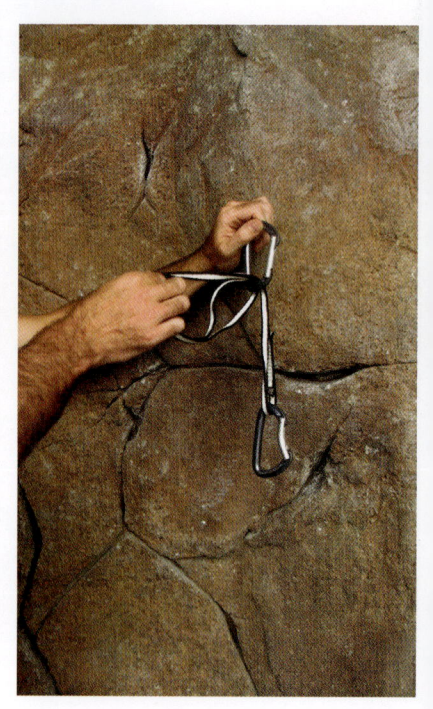

Extendable Quickdraws

You can extend your quickdraws in a few different ways: you can clip a few quickdraws together, or pull out one of your slings and clip that in with a couple of

TRAD CLIMBING 91

Clip the bottom snap-link through all three loops.

With the top snap-link attached to the gear, unclip the bottom snap link.

Re-clip the bottom snap-link to one loop of sling.

Pull it down to extend the sling.

snap links borrowed from a quickdraw (doing this while hanging off one arm can be difficult), or you can carry specific extendible quickdraws made up of two snap links and one 60cm sling.

Climbing with a 60cm quickdraw hanging off your harness is not practical, as it will swing around and get caught while you are climbing. So we fold it up as shown. In its longest position, pass the bottom snap link through the top one and then clip the bottom snap link to the two extra loops created. Both snap links will now be clipped to three loops.

To extend your quickdraw quickly, while hanging on with one hand, clip the gear as normal, then unclip the bottom snap link from all three loops of sling, re-clip it back to any one of the three loops and pull. The remaining loops will roll over the top snap link leaving you with a 60cm quickdraw in seconds.

Belay Stances: General Rules

A belay stance is anywhere that a climber stops, attaches themselves to the rock and brings their partner up to join them on top rope. How you attach yourself depends entirely on the surroundings and the gear you have left after your climb. Essentially, you will place a few bits of gear and attach them to your belay loop using a sling, the rope or a combination of the two.

JARGON

A belay: a place where you can attach yourself ready to hold the rope for your partner.
A belay stance: the same as a belay.
A belay device: a device used to control the rope as your partner climbs.
To belay: to hold the rope for your partner as they climb.
To build a belay: the act of attaching yourself to the rock ready to hold the rope for your climber.
Your belay position: the place that you stand or sit to hold the rope for your climber.

Score Your Belay Out of 20

When we looked at placing gear, we spoke about scoring your gear out of 10. So, a piece of gear that would only hold your car keys is 1/10 and a piece that would hold your car is 10/10. All the gear involved in your belay should add up to a total of at least 20. In other words, two bits of gear each 10/10 would be enough. Or three bits of gear – two 8/10s and one 5/10 – would also be enough. If you can only find 4/10 placements, you had better use at least five of them.

Anchor, Belayer, Climber (ABC)

The anchors (A), the belayer (B) and the climber (C) (or the last piece of protection) will come into a straight line when the climber falls off. You need to build your stance with this in mind. Already have yourself in the middle of this straight line when you tighten up the belay so that you do not get dragged around when your climber puts their weight on the rope.

Tighten Up the Belay

You should always try to be sitting or standing in a position where you can see and hear the climber coming up the route. This generally means sitting at the edge of the cliff. Make sure you tighten up the ropes holding you in place, otherwise you may find that you are pulled over the edge when your climber falls. This will shock load your gear and potentially be very uncomfortable.

ABC in line.

ABC out of line, if the climber falls, the belayer will be pulled to the side, mis-loading the belay.

GOOD, angle of 60 degrees.

BAD, angles over 90 degrees put extra load on each piece of gear.

DANGER, angles over 120 degrees hugely overload each piece of gear.

Angles and Redundancy

Each piece of gear needs to work independently of the other pieces in the belay, so you attach yourself to each piece of gear with a closed system that does not rely on any other piece. In other words, if one piece of gear fails, the other pieces should not be shock loaded but simply take up the load between them. How to achieve this will be shown in the examples below.

Each piece of gear will come together (at your harness or a knot) at an angle from each other. This angle will ideally be 60 degrees or less. Any angle between the gear will create extra load, as the gear will be pulled down by the climber and sideways by the other piece of protection. A very basic explanation of the physics of this is as follows: at 60 degrees, two pieces of gear holding a 100kg climber would be taking 58kg each. At 90 degrees, each piece would be taking 70kg and at 120 degrees, each would be taking 100kg, the full weight of the climber. Always aim

RIGHT: Make a mountain.

BELOW LEFT: Make a face.

BELOW RIGHT: Make another face.

TRAD CLIMBING

LEFT: Second face behind the first and clip both loops.

RIGHT: Hold the rope crossing the middle of the knot.

BELOW: Pull the rope out away from the knot.

for 60 degrees or less between each piece of gear. In practice you may have to stray from this optimum angle, but it is never a good idea to go beyond 90 degrees.

Belay Stances: The Clove Hitch

To make the belay stances described below, you will need to be able to tie a clove hitch. The clove hitch is usually the best knot to use, within a belay stance, as it is easily adjusted, so you can fine-tune your belay at any point to make sure all the above rules are in place.

Make a Mountain Holding the rope in both hands, make a hill (or mountain) shape away from you.

Make a Face Twist the right side of the mountain over the left side to create a circle (or face). These first two steps are the same as the first two steps of a figure-of-eight.

Make Another Face Still using your right hand, make an identical loop or face next to the first.

Second Face Behind The First Slot the second loop behind first loop and clip both loops to the carabiner.

Adjust the now loose knot in either direction.

Tighten Up The clove hitch is made up of two ropes going into the carabiner, with one rope crossing where the two ropes go in. Hold onto the crossing rope and pull it out so that the knot is now loose. From here you can adjust the knot easily by pulling and rolling the ropes over the carabiner.

Belay Stances: In-Reach, Using the Rope

In-reach means that all the gear you placed is within touching distance when you are standing or sitting in your final position. The normal procedure is to build the belay stance with a little slack in the system, then sit or stand where you are going to belay from and then tighten everything up. If you can reach the gear, this is nice and simple and the following methods work well.

Single-Point Belay (In-Reach, Using the Rope)

Let's imagine you have found a tree at the top of your route, not far from the edge, that would easily take the weight of two cars. You put a sling around the tree and this is now your single point of attachment.

You attach yourself, loosely, to the sling around the tree using a carabiner and a clove hitch in your rope. Sitting down into your final position, reach back to the sling and tighten up the clove hitch until the rope between you and the tree is taught. This is about as simple as belay stances get.

Double-Point Belay (In-Reach, Using the Rope)

This time your belay is made up of two pieces of gear that are both 10/10 and in-reach of your final belay position.

Clip the first piece of gear with a clove hitch from your figure-of-eight. Tighten it up so that you are secure in the final position you wish to be in

ABOVE LEFT: *Single point, in-reach, using the rope.*

ABOVE RIGHT: *Double point, in-reach, using the rope.*

BELOW RIGHT: *Triple point, in reach, using the rope.*

when you are belaying (this is the same as the single-point, in-reach method).

Using the slack rope coming out of the first piece of gear, tie another clove hitch and attach it to the second piece of protection. There should be some slack rope between these two pieces.

Now clove hitch the rope coming from the second piece of gear to a carabiner on your rope loop and tighten it up. You are now securely attached to two separate pieces.

Triple-Point Belay (In-Reach, Using the Rope)

On this occasion you have had to use three pieces of gear to get your total of 20/20. All the pieces are in-reach of your final position.

Attach yourself to the first two pieces of gear in exactly the same way as described above (in the Double-Point Belay, In-Reach, Using The Rope system).

TRAD CLIMBING

Single point, out-of-reach, using the rope.

Now take the loose rope coming from the clove hitch on your rope, loop back to the third piece of gear and attach it with another clove hitch. Tighten this final piece and you are good to go.

If you were using more than three in-reach pieces, you can simply keep repeating this process (with a clove hitch at every carabiner) until all the gear is attached and tightened up.

Belay Stances: Out-Of-Reach, Using the Rope

Out-of-reach means that the gear you placed is too far back from the edge to be reached when you are in your final belay position. If you use one of the methods above for in-reach belays, you will have to walk back and forth adjusting and re-adjusting your ropes in order to get the ropes tightened correctly. This will be frustrating, annoying and impractical. The following methods will make tightening up the ropes from your final belay position nice and simple.

Single-Point Belay (Out-Of-Reach, Using the Rope)

You have arrived at the top of your climb and found a solid 20/20 tree five metres back from the edge.

You walk up to the tree, put a sling around it and clip the rope through a carabiner on the sling. You then walk back to the edge of the cliff with the rope running through the carabiner.

Once you get to your final belay position (where you wish to sit), take the rope running up the route (back to the tree) and clove hitch it to a carabiner on your belay loop. You are now attached to your tree. The rope runs from your figure-of-eight, through the carabiner on the tree and back to a clove hitch on your rope loop.

Tighten up this clove hitch towards the tree and you are good to go.

Double-Point Belay (Out-Of-Reach, Using the Rope)

This time you find two pieces of gear far back from the edge of your cliff, which together add up to 20/20. They are both, however, out of reach once you are stood or sat at the edge.

Get the first piece of gear attached to your harness correctly, as described above with the single-point belay.

Now take the loose rope coming from the clove hitch on your harness back to the second piece of gear, run it through a carabiner and come back to your belay position.

Take the rope running up the route back to the second piece and clove hitch it to the carabiner on your rope loop (the same one you used to attach yourself to the first piece). You now have two separate closed loops, one for each piece of gear.

TRAD CLIMBING

Double point, out-of-reach, using the rope.

Triple point, out-of-reach, using the rope, method one.

RIGHT: *Figure-of-eight, on the bight.*

Triple-Point Belay (Out-Of-Reach, Using the Rope): Method 1

Essentially you can use the exact same system as the double-point system but with one extra piece of gear. You simply repeat the process over and over until all the gear is attached by large loops to your harness.

To stop you walking back and forth to your gear, try clipping the rope through all the gear and then clipping the loops in between back through a carabiner on your harness. Now you should be able to walk back to the edge, dragging the rope loops with you. Then once you have sat down you can take the loops out and clove hitch them back into the carabiner.

Triple-Point Belay (Out-Of-Reach, Using the Rope): Method 2

The potential problem with method one is that it uses a lot of rope. If you are at the top of the crag, and can walk around with no danger of falling off the edge, then you may wish to use a different method.

Untie your figure-of-eight and attach this to your first piece of gear with a new figure-of-eight on the bight.

A little way down the rope, tie an overhand knot with a loop large enough to reach the second piece of gear. Make sure the loop and the rope are at 60 degrees to each other and that both are taut. Repeat this process with any more pieces of protection required.

100 TRAD CLIMBING

TOP LEFT: *Make a loop in the rope.*

TOP RIGHT *Pass the loop around the back of both ropes.*

BELOW LEFT *Pull the knot tight and clip back to the carabiner.*

Walk to within a few metres of the edge and loosely clove hitch the rope to your belay loop with a carabiner. Leave yourself enough slack to get to and sit down at the edge of the cliff. Go and sit down and tighten up the clove hitch until you are held tightly in place by the belay.

Belay Stances: Using a Sling

Slings can be used to bring your gear together in the same way as the rope. You will need different sized slings, depending on how far away each piece is and how many pieces there are in the system.

TRAD CLIMBING   101

Triple point, out-of-reach, using the rope, method two.

TRAD CLIMBING

Double-Point Belay (Using A Sling): Method 1

Clip the sling to both pieces of gear, preferably using screw-gate carabiners (snap links will do the same job if you have run out but be careful as they can open when pressed against rock making them much weaker, two snap links back to back is safer).

Now bring the piece of sling running between the two bits of gear down to meet the bottom of the sling.

Tie an overhand knot on the bight to create a single, equalized attachment point. You can now attach yourself to this loop.

Double-Point Belay (Using A Sling): Method 2

Tie a loose overhand knot in the middle of your sling and clip either end to your two pieces of gear.

Move the overhand knot until it sits at the base of the sling (or wherever you need it to sit, so that the ABC is in line).

Clip a carabiner through each side of the knot separately, and attach yourself to this carabiner.

Clip the sling to both carabiners.

Bring the sling into two loops, one inside the other.

Double point, using a sling, method one.

TRAD CLIMBING 103

Tie an overhand in the sling and clip both ends.

Bring to the knot in to line with ABC.

Clip both loops either side of the knot.

Double point, using a sling, method two.

104 TRAD CLIMBING

TOP LEFT: *Clip the sling through all the gear.*

TOP RIGHT: *Bring down the sling between the carabiners.*

BELOW RIGHT: *Bring all three loops down together.*

Triple-Point Belay (Using A Sling)

If you have a long enough sling, you can bring together three or more pieces of gear to a single loop.

Clip your sling through all the gear.

Bring down both pieces of sling running between the gear, so that you end up with two loops hanging in the middle and one on the outside (three loops in total).

Finally, tie all these loops together in one large overhand knot at the base, clip to this single equalized attachment point and you are done.

Belay Stances: Combining Rope, Sling, In- and Out-Of-Reach

In the real world you will have to combine the methods above together to create solid belays as you see fit. You may have two out-of-reach placements and one in-reach. You may decide to use two pieces of gear far away from the edge, together with a sling, and then clip the sling as a single out-of-reach point. These methods are the basics and will need to be combined depending on the situation.

Belay Stances: Direct or Indirect?

All the methods described above are indirect belays. This is where you are attached directly to the anchor and the belay device is attached to your rope loop. The indirect refers to the weight of the climber going through the belayer's rope loop before going through belay.

A direct belay is where your belay device is attached to a single equalized attachment point directly, and is not attached to your harness. This means that the weight of the climber goes straight into the gear and does not pass through your body. This is much more comfortable, but there are disadvantages. You will need the belay device to be either a magic plate of some sort (such as the PETZL reverso) or an Italian hitch (see Chapter 11 for details) and it needs to be hanging freely in the air in order to be manipulated properly. Plus your gear has to be totally bomb proof.

The main advantage of the indirect system is that, by sitting at the edge in a strong position with the ropes holding you tightly in place, you add strength to the belay. When people first started climbing, this was often all they had and would just sit strong and belay with no gear at all. I am not suggesting you do this but know that sitting in a strong position adds about five points to your belay. If you can only get 15/20, then an indirect belay is essential.

Triple point, using a sling.

If you are in a hanging belay, as can happen in multi-pitch climbing, there is no difference between direct and indirect, as all the weight will come onto the gear either way. It is probably best to go with a direct belay in this situation as it will be more comfortable and, as there is nowhere to stand or sit, you would not be able to add any strength to the belay using your body anyway.

BELAY STANCES: IN SHORT

- Score your gear out of 20.
- ABC in a straight line.
- Tighten up the belay once in position.
- Aim for angles of 60 degrees or less.

Communication

Climbing Calls

When arriving at your belay stance, you may find that communication is difficult with your partner. This is typically because you have climbed around a corner of rock, or the wind is blowing or some other less aesthetic reason, such as a

TRAD CLIMBING

Magic plate set up for a direct belay.

> **COMMUNICATION: IN SHORT**
>
> - Top: Safe.
> - Bottom: Off belay.
> - Bottom: That's me (when the rope is tight).
> - Top: On belay, climb when you're ready.
> - Bottom: Climbing.
> - Top: OK.
>
> Practice rope tugging in advance.

nearby road. It is essential that you have some basic simple calls that can be used to communicate when a long sentence would be lost to the wind. The usual method in the UK is as follows:

- Climber arrives at the belay station, builds their belay and gets themselves attached to the rock. They then shout: **'Safe'**.
- The belayer hears this and takes the rope out of their belay device. They then shout: **'Off belay'**.
- The person at the top of the climb then knows that they can start pulling in all the excess slack. Once the climber at the bottom feels the rope pulling on their harness, they shout up: **'That's me'**.
- At that point, the person at the top puts the climber on belay and lets the climber know that they are ready by shouting: **'On belay, climb when you're ready'**.
- The climber at the bottom sorts out any last jobs (undoing their belay if they are multi-pitching, doing up their shoes, etc.) and then shouts: **'Climbing'**.
- The belayer, begins to take-in and answers: **'OK'**.

Non-Verbal Communication

Sometimes verbal communication is impossible and in these cases it is best to have a rope-pulling system. If you think about it, there are only two vital pieces of information you need: when you can take your climber off belay, and when you are on belay and can start climbing. These bits of information can be conveyed using rope tugs as described below:

- After arriving at the top and making yourselves safe, you indicate this to your belayer by tugging on the rope sharply three times. Make sure these tugs are clear and confident and will not be mistaken for normal climbing movements (TUG TUG TUG).
- The belayer feels this and takes you off belay. At the top you wait a few moments to give the belayer a chance to take the rope out of their belay plate before pulling up the excess slack. Once the rope comes tight you put the person at the bottom on belay and give three hard tugs on the rope (TUG TUG TUG).
- The climber at the bottom now understands that they are on belay and begins to climb.

It is best to use this system with a partner you know well. It is also advisable to practise this system so that you do not mistake a gentle tug for the wrong thing and take the climber off just as they are about to make the crux moves.

You could use two-way radios but, unless you are in Yosemite, this is just not cool. Plus, when your batteries run out...

> **JARGON**
>
> **Back-to-back snap links:** two snap links used together but facing opposite directions.
> **Chock stone:** a rock wedged in a crack.
> **Haul-loop:** some harnesses have a loop at the back of the waist belt designed to carry up a spare rope.
> **Seconding:** top roping up a route to join your partner while removing their gear.
> **Turn the lip:** climbing past the edge of an overhang, after which the rock is at a significantly easier angle.

CHAPTER 11
MULTI-PITCH CLIMBING

Trystan Jones Morris pitch 15 on the Lotus Flower Tower, Canada. © JACK GRIFFITHS

Multi-Pitch Kit List
Trad or Sport Kit

See trad or sport kit list for details. Even if you are multi-pitch sport climbing, you should carry a couple of prusiks and slings for abseiling or emergencies (see Chapters 12 and 13 for details).

Headtorch

A lightweight headtorch should live in your bag for emergencies. Not having a torch can turn an easy walk out into an epic and dangerous nightmare, and abseiling in complete darkness is not advisable.

A lightweight powerful head torch is essential on a long route.

Water Bottle

You are likely to want to take a water bottle up the route with you. With a little ingenuity, and some string, you can clip any bottle to your harness, if you do not want to carry a rucksack. However, a purpose-made one will generally be more hard-wearing.

MULTI-PITCH CLIMBING

A solid water-bottle that can be clipped to your harness can be useful.

Small Rucksack

If your route will take more than a few hours, you are likely to want to take a few items in a small rucksack up your route. Try to get a small sack that has a little rigidity and can be tightened up close to your body. A water bottle banging around in a massive bag behind you is likely to throw you off balance. Also, the tendency is to fill any bag you take. A 20ltr bag should be enough for a jacket, some food, water and a headtorch.

What to Carry Up Your Route?

It is a good idea to ask yourself the following questions before heading off:

- How long do I think this route will take?
- What is the weather forecast?
- How easy is it to get off the route if we run into trouble?
- When we get to the top do we walk down or abseil?

Let's imagine that the answers are: it will take us three hours, the forecast is good, we can abseil down the route at any time and plan to abseil down once we have finished the route. In this case, a few cereal bars in our pockets, a litre of water hanging off the second's harness and a headtorch will be all the extra kit we need to bring. No need for a rucksack.

Now let's imagine the answers are: it will take twelve hours if all goes well, the forecast is good but it will be cold at night, retreat would be complicated and we intend to walk down from the summit. In this case, you may wish to bring significant extra warm clothing, extra food and water, a pair of shoes to walk down in and, of course, a headtorch.

The trouble with the second kind of route is that the likelihood of being benighted is quite high and no one likes sleeping on a small ledge, spooning their mate to keep warm. The temptation is to bring a sleeping bag, food for two days and other luxuries, but all this extra kit will be heavy and will slow you down. This reduction in your pace means you are more likely to get caught out in the first place.

How long your route will take you depends on your ability, the route and how much you carry. A good pace is thirty minutes per pitch. This means ten minutes climbing, each, and ten minutes for building belays and changeovers. This is a good pace to aim for but, if the route is close to your limit and has some complicated route-finding, then an hour or more per pitch may be more realistic.

MULTI-PITCH KIT LIST: IN SHORT

- Always carry a headtorch.
- The lighter you are, the faster you will climb.
- Get a small, close-fitting rucksack for spare kit.
- Ask the questions above, before you set off.

The speed at which you climb between belay stances can be improved by carrying less and/or placing less gear. The overall time you spend on your route can be vastly reduced by quick and efficient changeovers. If your route is twelve pitches long and you spend an extra five minutes chatting (or sorting something out) at every belay, then that is one full extra hour on the route!

How It Works

You and your mate plan your day the night before. You plan what to take with you, depending on how long the route will take, the weather conditions and the information in the guidebook. In the morning, after walking up to the base of your route, you decide to take the first pitch. At the top of the first pitch you find a place to build a belay stance, attach yourself to the rock and bring your mate up on top rope. Once they arrive, you spend a couple of minutes sorting out the kit and then your partner heads off up the next pitch. You repeat this process (swinging leads) until you get to the top. If your route has an abseil descent, then you can abseil straight back to the ground. Alternatively, you can put on your trainers and walk back down.

Swinging Leads or Block Leading?

The method described above is a standard British way of multi-pitching and is referred to as swinging leads. This means that you will second (top rope) up to your mate removing their gear, arrive at the belay to sort out the rack and then straight away start leading the next pitch. If these pitches are long, you could easily end up climbing for a hundred metres or more in one virtually continuous push. Although this can feel great, if both pitches are hard, then this is a potentially poor tactic. Swinging leads is a very elegant and simple method of multi-pitch climbing and as routes in the UK are rarely more than four or five pitches long, it is regularly used.

Many routes in mainland Europe and in the US are best done by block leading. This means that one climber will lead a block of say six pitches and then their partner will lead the next six. The advantage of this is that you only ever climb for one pitch before having a rest. It is also a way of saving the stronger climber for the harder pitches (just like the team riders in the tour de France will protect their strongest finisher).

In Yosemite and other large granite crags in the US it is typical to block lead and for the second to ascend the rope on Jumars (mechanical ascenders), rather than climb on top rope. This can save a vast amount of time, which is key when you have one thousand metres to climb in one day. The tactics used for big walling, as it is called, are varied and complex and not covered in this book. If you are heading out to Yosemite, you may find that normal free-climbing techniques will not be sufficient for you to achieve your goals. I suggest getting a specific book on the subject and/or finding an experienced guide to teach you the necessary techniques.

Changeovers

At each changeover, the climber will need to make sure the rack is organized correctly on their harness. The belayer will need to be sure that the rope is ready to pay out to the climber before they start up the next pitch. If you are on a large ledge, this is nice and easy; however, if you are at a hanging belay, then it can require a little more thought to ensure a slick changeover.

Rope Organization

If you are belaying from a large ledge, simply pile your rope up on top of itself as your climber comes up underneath you. Once they arrive, their end of the rope will be at the top and yours will be at the bottom. If they are leading the next pitch,

Brenden Harkness showing good rope work, each loop being lapped over his harness and each one smaller than the last. © JACK GRIFFITHS

MULTI-PITCH CLIMBING

then you do not need to do anything with the rope as it should pay out off the top of the pile easily. If you are block leading, however, you will need to feed the rope into a new pile to ensure that the climber's end of the rope is on top.

If you are on a hanging belay, you will need to loop the rope over the rope or sling attaching you to the belay. The problem with this method is that loops can get caught inside one another, which can create tangles in the rope. You can avoid this by making each loop shorter than the one before. If your first loop is 4m long, then the next loop should be 3.5m long. In this way, when you come to take up the 3.5m-loop, there is no way it can reach down and hook over the loop below. If block leading on a hanging stance, get your belayer to re-loop the rope over their cow's tail (or rope), attaching them to the belay before you head off.

Belay Device Orientation

If you are belaying from your harness, with your device correctly orientated to bring up your second, then it is likely that you will have to turn the device around in order to belay smoothly, once they are above you. It would be ideal for your climber to attach themselves to the belay as you change it over but if this is impractical, simply put an overhand knot in the dead rope, attach this to your belay loop and then turn the belay device around. Remember, it is important that you are able to lock off away from the climber. If they are heading out to your right, you will need to belay left-handed. If you belay with the dead rope towards your climber, then it is much harder to lock off the device properly, should they fall.

Arrange Your Belay for a Lead Fall

If your climber is much heavier than you, it is worth placing a piece of gear below you to take an upward pull. It is possible for a heavy climber to lift a smaller belayer completely off the belay stance and for all the gear to come out with them.

An overhand knot in the dead rope and attached to the rope loop allows the belay device to be removed and adjusted.

One extra piece will stop the original sling belay from being mis-loaded if the leader falls off.

MULTI-PITCH CLIMBING

Simple block swap from a sling belay. For demonstration purposes, the red rope is the second's and the blue rope is the leader's.

Both climbers are attached to the same gear with their ends of the rope. For demonstration purposes, the red rope is the second's and the blue rope is the leader's.

If your climber is heading out left from the belay, make sure that your belay is set up for a leftward pull. One piece of solid gear to the right of you should be enough to stop you swinging across and loading your original belay incorrectly.

Changeovers for Swinging Leads

If you are swinging leads, then there is no real need for the climber arriving at the belay stance to attach themselves to the belay. So long as they have a small ledge to stand on, you can put an overhand knot in the dead rope and pass them all the gear. Adjust the belay device, if necessary, and they can head on up the route. If you do not have a small ledge, the climber will need to attach themselves to the belay in order to be hands-free while sorting out the rack.

> **CHANGEOVERS: IN SHORT**
>
> Before you leave the belay stance, make sure:
>
> - The climber's end of the rope is at the top of the pile.
> - The belay device is orientated correctly (dead rope away from the climber).
> - The belay stance can take a pull from the direction of the leading climber (if necessary).

Changeovers for Block Leads

If you are changing the belayer and the climber over, then the climber will need to attach themselves to the belay stance. If you have set this up with a sling belay, with one equalized attachment point, then this is nice and simple. Both of you attach to this point, re-flake the rope and off you go.

If you have built the belay using the rope, then this is slightly more complicated. The climber arriving at the belay stance clips into the gear underneath your attachments and builds the same belay, making sure to always keep their rope underneath yours. When you start climbing, you will find your ropes

MULTI-PITCH CLIMBING

on top and clear of the belayer's anchors. Problems occur when the ropes are not kept completely separate.

Italian Hitch

The Italian hitch is a rolling knot that can be used to belay or abseil with. It is the get-out-of-jail-free knot if you drop your belay device, and can also be a very comfortable way to belay someone directly from a single, equalized attachment point. Be aware though that using an Italian hitch does twist up the rope, so it is best not to use it all the time.

Make a Mountain Holding the rope in both hands, make a hill (or mountain) shape away from you.

Make a face Twist the right side of the mountain over the left side to create a circle (or face).

Make Another Face Still using your right hand, make an identical loop or face next to the original. These first three steps are the same as for the clove hitch.

TOP RIGHT: *Make a mountain.*

BELOW LEFT: *Make a face.*

BELOW RIGHT: *Make another face.*

MULTI-PITCH CLIMBING 113

Close it like a book.

Clip both loops.

Close It Like a Book Close the two loops together like you would close a book.

Clip Both Loops Clip both of the loops to a pear-shaped carabiner (they are much harder to manipulate in D-shaped carabiners).

Direct Belay With an Italian Hitch

The main difference between belaying with an Italian hitch and a belay plate is that the Italian hitch is locked off towards the climber. This is what makes it ideal for belaying when you are standing below the belay stance. The technique is just to pull it through and swap your hands, as necessary, making sure you always hold onto the dead rope.

Magic Plates

There are a few devices on the market that have the advantage of locking-off automatically when used directly from the belay. They are basically the same as a regular tubular device, but with an extra attachment point at the top of the plate. This gets attached to the equalized attachment point and you simply pull the rope (or ropes) through the device. If your climber falls off, the rope on top will pull the free-hanging carabiner into the device hard enough to arrest the fall for you – leaving you free to eat your sandwiches.

Releasing a Magic Plate

A common problem with magic plates is lowering a climber down, once the device has locked-off. Should your partner be hanging in space and wish to be lowered, then you will need to be able to release the magic plate safely.

Backup the Plate First, you need to backup the magic plate with an Italian hitch in the dead rope attached to your belay loop (it doesn't have to be an Italian hitch, any belay device will do but you probably won't have another one spare).

Create the Pulley System Use a lark's foot to attach a sling to the free-hanging carabiner (the carabiner locking the rope in the magic plate). Run that sling up through a higher attachment point and back to your belay loop.

ITALIAN HITCH: IN SHORT

- Make two loops and close it like a book.
- Always hold onto the dead rope.
- Lock off towards the climber.

114 MULTI-PITCH CLIMBING

Magic plate set up for a direct belay.

Fall Factor 2

Let's imagine you are multi-pitch climbing. You left your belay stance and climbed 10m above your belayer without placing any gear. If you fell off, you would fall past your belayer until you were 10m below them. This would be a fall of 20m on 10m of rope, which gives a fall factor of 2.

20m fall ÷ 10m rope = fall factor 2.

A factor 2 fall is horrendous. People I have spoken to who have taken one, or seen someone take one, liken them to a car crash. They put a massive load through the climber's body, potentially breaking their hips and causing internal injuries. The forces are so high that carabiners and other equipment have been known to break. Factor 2 falls of any size are to be avoided.

Sit Back and Lower Keeping hold of the dead rope coming out of the Italian hitch, sit down into your harness. This should pull the magic plate's free-hanging carabiner up, releasing the magic plate completely. You can now lower the climber using the Italian hitch on your harness.

Fall Factors

Fall factors measure the potential severity of a fall. They are calculated using the following equation:

Fall distance ÷ rope in the system = fall factor.

Backup the plate.

MULTI-PITCH CLIMBING

Create the pulley system.

Sit back and lower.

Fall Factor 1.6

Now let's imagine that you have left the belay stance and put in a piece of gear immediately, say 2m from your belayer's belay device, and then climbed up a further 8m without placing any gear. If you fell off now it would create a fall factor of 1.6:

16m fall ÷ 10m rope = fall factor 1.6.

A fall facture of 1.6 is significantly less than a fall factor of 2. The forces are massively reduced just by putting in one piece of gear just above the belay. Any fall where you pass your belayer (in other words fall factors above 1) is not going to be a pleasant experience, but a factor 2 is vastly worse than a fall factor 1.9. The moral of the story is to get some gear in as soon as you leave the belay. Sometimes you may even use a piece of gear that is currently being used for the belay stance, so long as the belay stance as a whole is not compromised.

Fall Factor 1

This time you leave your belay stance and place a few bits of gear up to 5m from your belayer. You then climb up a further 5m until you are 10m above them. If you fall off now you will arrive back next to your belayer having taken a factor 1 fall:

10m fall ÷ 10m rope = fall factor 1.

A factor 1 fall is as big an impact as you would want to take. Anything over 1 will leave a mark. A factor 1 fall will not be fun but is unlikely to generate enough force to break anything, so long as you do not swing into the wall.

Fall Factor 0.6

Finally, let's look at a fall you are more likely to take. Let's imagine you leave the belayer and place gear all the way up to 7m, you then climb a further 3m and fall off. The fall will be 6m long with 10m of rope out, giving you a fall factor of 0.6:

6m fall ÷ 10m rope = fall factor 0.6.

116 MULTI-PITCH CLIMBING

Fall factor 2	Fall factor 1.6	Fall factor 1	Fall factor 0.6
No gear	Gear 2m	Gear 5m	Gear 7m
Live rope 10m	Live rope 10m	Live rope 10m	Live rope 10m
Fall 20m	Fall 16m	Fall 10m	Fall 6m

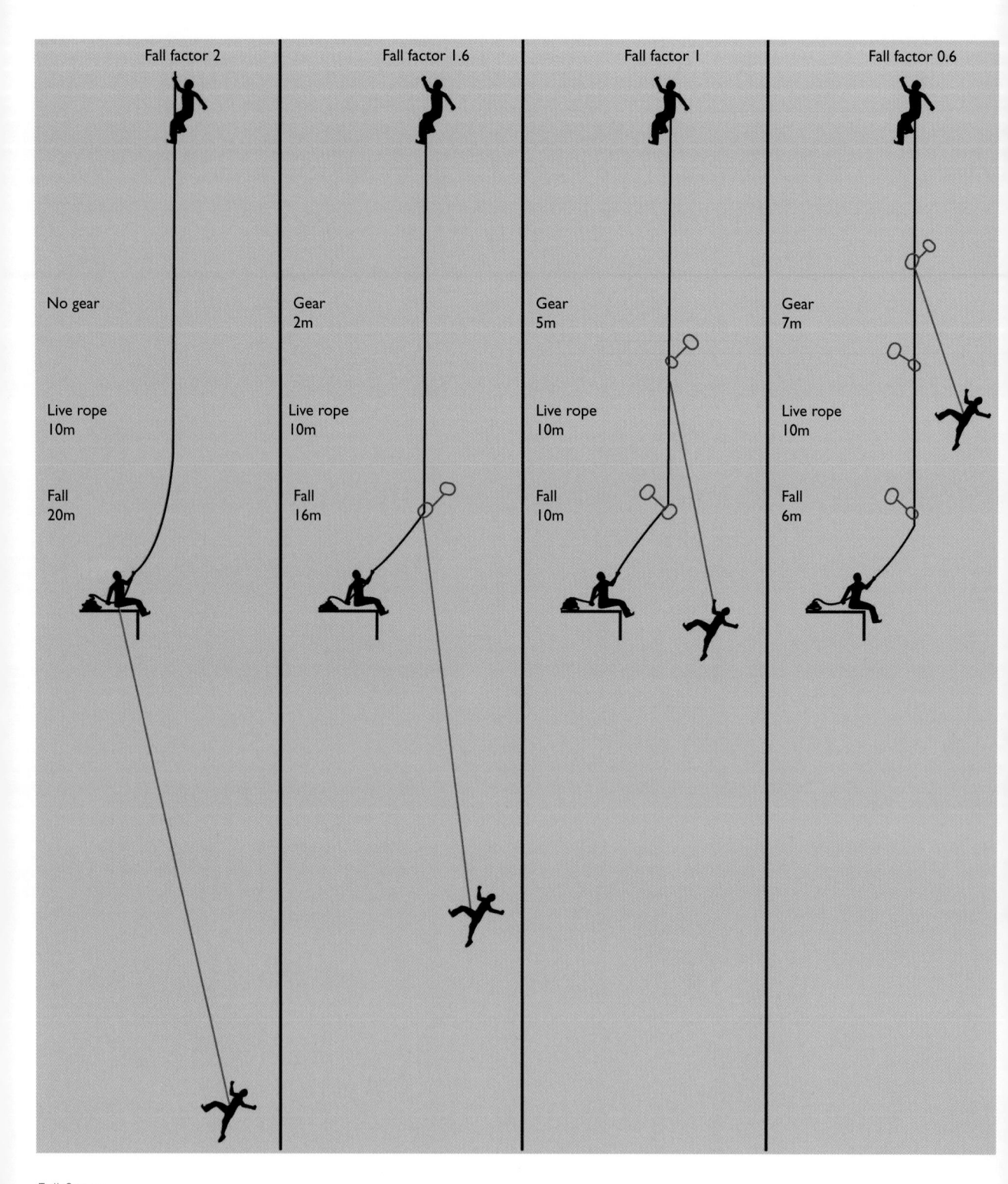

Fall factors.

MULTI-PITCH CLIMBING

FALL FACTORS: IN SHORT

- Place some gear soon after leaving the belay stance.
- Dynamic belaying can dampen the forces involved.
- Fall distance ÷ rope length = fall factor.

All your equipment is happy to take this type of fall. This sort of distance may shake up a climber but, so long as everything works as it should, you just get back on the wall and carry on climbing. Falling off is part of the game and so long as you avoid falls over a factor of 1, then they should only dent your ego.

The reality is that fall factors are not the full story. Your rope will stretch, the knots will tighten up, the belayer will be lifted up or react as discussed in the dynamic belaying section, and much of the force goes elsewhere. The main thing to avoid is a fall factor of 2, which could cause you a lot of trouble, but is avoidable by placing some gear close to the belay.

JARGON

Benighted: an unplanned night spent outdoors.
Changeovers: anywhere where both climbers come together at a belay and swap some gear over.
Free climbing: only using your body to gain height and only using the equipment to protect a fall.
Hanging belay: a belay stance with no ledge to stand on.
Jumars: mechanical ascenders, used for climbing ropes.
The second: the climber who climbs the pitch on top rope, removing the leader's gear.

CHAPTER 12

ABSEILING

Abseiling Kit List

You should be able to set up an abseil, and lower yourself down it, with the kit you normally take to the crag. However, sea-cliff crags can require a very long abseil approach and you may also wish to leave this rope in place so you can get back to the top in an emergency. In this case, a spare, long, static rope would be a wise purchase.

Trad or Sport Kit

See kit list Chapter 9 or 10 for details.

Prusik and D-Shaped Carabiner

See Chapter 10 for details of prusiks and Chapter 8 for carabiner descriptions.

120cm Sling

See Chapter 10 for details of slings. A 120cm sling can be used to extend the abseiling device away from your body and to clip yourself into abseil stations when doing multiple abseils. Details described later in this chapter.

Static Rope (Low-Stretch Rope)

Climbing rope is dynamic, which means it stretches (by approximately 10 per cent of its length) under load. When you are abseiling, this stretching means that you bounce a little (or a lot if you are near the end of the rope). If your rope is running over a sharp edge of rock, this bouncing can easily damage the rope or even cut straight through it.

Author abseiling in the Peak District, UK.

ABSEILING

BUYING ABSEILING KIT

- You should be able to abseil with your standard rack.
- You need at least one prusik.
- Consider a static rope if you intend to regularly climb on sea cliffs.

You can buy low-stretch ropes (called static ropes but in reality they just stretch less than a dynamic rope), which reduce this bouncing effect, making abseiling easier and safer. I am not suggesting you carry a separate rope for abseiling up every route you do, but if you often go to a crag that requires an abseil approach (such as a sea cliff), then investing in a static rope would be advisable.

Fixed Abseils

Abseiling has become an 'adventure activity' with many people abseiling for charity or as part of an activity weekend. Abseiling on your own, however, should be taken very seriously. You are placing your life completely in your own ability to place gear and build solid abseil stations.

What is a Fixed Abseil?

A fixed abseil is a fixed line where the top of the rope is attached to the top of the cliff and the rest of the rope trails down to the ground. To get your rope back once you have completed your abseil, you will have to walk or climb back to the top in order to dismantle the system and retrieve your gear.

When to Set Up a Fixed Abseil?

Fixed abseils are used mainly at single-pitch venues to retrieve some stuck gear, to inspect a route before climbing, to rescue a climber in difficulties or, in the case of sea cliffs, to get to the start of your route. Abseiling at a single-pitch venue is rarely completely necessary, unless you are at a sea cliff venue.

Abseiling on a Fixed Line

To attach yourself to a fixed line you will need a belay device, a pear-shaped carabiner, a prusik and a D-shaped carabiner.

Attach Everything to Yourself Clip the belay device to your belay loop using the pear-shaped carabiner. Now lark's foot the prusik to your leg loop and clip the D-shaped carabiner to the same leg loop (slightly higher than the prusik so that it doesn't fall around the back of the harness).

Attach the Prusik to the Rope Take the prusik around the rope three times

Pass the prusik behind the leg loop.

ABSEILING

LEFT: Pass one end of the prusik through the other.

BELOW: Pull it in tight.

(you may find you need more or fewer turns, depending on rope thickness) and clip it back to the carabiner on your leg loop.

Attach Your Belay Device to the Rope Bring up some slack through the prusik and attach the device as though you where about to belay, with the 'live rope' running towards the anchors.

Check It Check yourself as though you were the belayer. In other words, check that your harness is doubled back, that your belay device is correctly attached and that the screw gate is done up. If possible, abseil a short way down the rope while still clipped in with a long sling to make sure your setup is working.

ABSEILING 121

Hanging Around

The prusik is there to act as a backup to your hand. If a falling rock knocks you unconscious, then the prusik should stop you from falling too far down the rope. However, it is not a complete backup. If you have to stop to sort something out (collect some gear or untangle a rope), then put a few turns of the dead rope around your leg to backup the prusik.

Questions About Prusiks

You may ask why the prusik is attached to your leg loop and not the belay loop. To unlock a prusik, you press down on the

ABOVE: *Attach the prusik to the rope.*

RIGHT: *Attach your belay device to the rope.*

top of it, this releases the prusik allowing the rope to slide through. If the prusik is allowed to get too close and touch the belay device, the plate of the belay device can release the prusik making it useless. So we need some distance between the prusik and the device. Some people will extend their belay device away from them with a sling to keep this distance. This can work well but be sure that the sling does not twist, as this causes the rope to twist around the sling, which makes abseiling very difficult.

You may also ask why it is attached below the belay device rather than above. The prusik should act very much like a second hand. It is underneath the belay device so that it does not need to take all the weight of the climber should they suddenly let go; it only needs to bite enough to make the belay device do its job.

Fixed Abseil Setup

The easiest setup is very similar to a method discussed in Chapter 10.

Get Good Gear

First of all, get two or three bits of gear that are bomb proof. You want your abseil to add up to at least 20/20.

Attach and Equalize the Gear with the Rope

Tie a figure-of-eight and clip it to the piece of gear furthest away from the edge. A little way down the rope, tie an overhand knot with a loop large enough to reach the second piece of gear. Make sure the loop and the rope are at 60 degrees to each other and that both are taut to the gear. Repeat this process with any more gear, as required.

A potentially easier method (requiring good gear close together) is to build a belay with a sling and simply attach one end of the rope to the single equalized attachment point with a figure-of-eight on the bight.

Abseiler has two turns around their leg to backup the prusik.

ABSEILING

Fixed abseil set up, using the rope.

Fixed abseil set up, using a sling.

Knot the End and Throw the Rope

The other end of the rope (the one being thrown to the bottom of your crag) should be knotted to prevent you abseiling off the end, should your rope be too short. A stopper knot works well with most devices, but if you are using a figure-of-eight descender, you will need a bigger knot.

The rest of the rope can now be thrown over the edge. It is courteous to shout 'below' before throwing the rope down, to warn anyone below that they may be hit by your rope or small stones it may dislodge.

Pad Out the Edge

You should always protect the rope from abrasion over any point that the rope takes a sharp angle over rock. You can use a rucksack or jumper, or you can buy specific rope protectors. Always build your abseil assuming you will have to prusik back up it later (prusiking up a rope is discussed in the next chapter).

FIXED ABSEILS: IN SHORT

- Be sure your anchors are solid.
- Pad out sharp edges.
- Knot the end of the rope.
- Check everything before you commit.

Retrievable Abseils

A retrievable abseil is a method of abseiling that allows you to retrieve your rope once you get to your next abseil station, or back to the ground.

A stopper knot in the end works well.

ABSEILING

When to Set Up a Retrievable Abseil?

A typical reason to set up a retrievable abseil is that your rope is not long enough to get to the ground in one go. If you are 100m up your route, and your rope is 50m long, a fixed abseil will only get you half-way back down the crag. So we need a method to be able to do multiple abseils, which means we will need to retrieve our rope after every abseil so we can use it again.

How Does It Work?

By clipping the middle of your rope to your abseil station, you can attach yourself to both sides of the rope using the two holes in your belay device. In this way you are weighting both sides of the rope going through the anchor. Once you get to the bottom, you pull on one side of the rope and the other side will thread through the anchor and fall down the crag, you now have your rope back.

How Far Can You Abseil?

With the retrievable method, you can abseil half the length of your rope in one go. If you have one 60m rope you can abseil 30m. If you have two 60m ropes, by tying the ends together you essentially have a 120m rope and can therefore abseil up to 60m at a time. However, as you can retrieve your rope, you can abseil again and again until you get back down to the ground.

What Do You Attach Your Rope To?

In a perfect world you will have abseil stations down your crag every 30m. If you are multi-pitch sport climbing, then this is more than likely, as an abseil station is essentially the same as a lower-off. If you are trad climbing, then you may have to use some natural features. Often there are bits of tat (old

The edge padded out to protect the rope.

ropes and slings) threaded around spikes and trees down crags that have popular abseil descents. However, if the in situ gear is poor, or non-existent, you may be forced to leave some gear behind in order to get down safely.

While retreating off a twenty-eight pitch route in the Dolomites, after being caught in the rain, my partner and I left the majority of our rack behind in order to get off safely. This cost us a lot of money but we are here to tell the tale. Many people have lost their lives trying to abseil off something that is less than one hundred per cent solid.

If what you find to abseil off is not ideal, or is hard to inspect, you may wish to back it up with some of your own gear. Sometimes, just for peace of mind, it is good to backup the abseil and let the heavier person go down first with all the kit, while the lighter person watches how the gear behaves. If they are satisfied that it is safe, they can remove the backup and follow on; if not, the backup stays in and the gear is sacrificed.

Attaching Yourself to a Retrievable Abseil

The method described for fixed abseiling, works just as well for a retrievable abseil, with just a couple of alterations. First, make sure that both ropes go through your belay plate – abseiling off one would be almost undoubtedly fatal. Second, you will need a cow's tail on you in order to attach yourself to the abseil stations, as you come down your route.

You can add a small knot in your cow's tail, about 15cm (6in), in front of your harness, in order to extend your belay device away from the prusik and have a cow's tail available in one clean system. This is the best practice system but if it confuses you, just use the fixed line set up with a separate cow's tail.

Multiple Abseil Setup (Using Double Ropes)

Thread One Rope Thread the end of one of your ropes (the blue rope in this

126 ABSEILING

example) through the anchor and then tie both ropes together with an overhand knot about a metre from the end of the rope. If your ropes are different diameters, use a fisherman's knot, as with your prusiks, or multiple overhands. This knot should sit clear of the anchor. You will pull this knot down later, so be sure there is nothing to get in its way.

Cow's tail and extended belay device in one system.

Thread one rope.

ABSEILING

Knot the Ends and Throw the Ropes
Put a stopper knot in the ends of both ropes (a stopper knot works well with most devices, but if you are using a figure-of-eight descender, you will need a bigger knot). Throw the ropes down the crag after shouting 'below'.

Attach Yourself, Check It and Abseil Down Attach your belay device and prusik to the abseil ropes, test it while you are still loosely attached to the anchor with a cow's tail and then abseil down to your next abseil station.

ABOVE: *Knot the ends and throw the ropes.*
© JACK GRIFFITHS

BELOW: *Shout 'below' and throw.* © JACK GRIFFITHS

128 ABSEILING

Attach yourself, check it and abseil down.

The end of the red rope is threaded through the new anchor and knotted.
© JACK GRIFFITHS

130 ABSEILING

The red rope is pulled down until the knot attaching the two ropes is at the new abseil station. © JACK GRIFFITHS

The knot at the bottom of the blue rope is removed and the blue rope pulled all the way down. © JACK GRIFFITHS

ABSEILING

> **RETRIEVABLE ABSEILS: IN SHORT**
> - If in doubt, backup your anchors (leave gear if necessary).
> - Knot the ends of both ropes.
> - Keep the rope attached to something solid at all times.
> - Check yourself before you commit.

Remove Knots, Thread Anchor and Pull Rope When you are both at the next anchor, remove the knots from the bottom of your ropes and thread the red rope through your new abseil station and re-tie the knot in the end. Pull the red rope down, through the anchor, until the knot tying both ropes together comes all the way down. Now pull the blue rope until it falls all the way down the crag. It is worth getting hold of the end of the blue rope and putting a knot in it, unless you are certain it reaches the ground.

You can continue this process until you run out of cliff. You will pull alternately on blue and then red and so on all the way down. A good piece of advice is to always have the rope attached to something solid (e.g. belay loop or the anchor). You do not want to pull your rope through only for it to fall to the floor leaving you halfway up the crag.

The new abseil station is now set up and ready to use (remember to put a knot at the end of the blue rope). © JACK GRIFFITHS

> **JARGON**
>
> **Abseil station:** a place to attach your rope in order to abseil (the same as a lower-off if sport climbing).
> **Anchor:** any solid point that a climber uses to attach themselves to the rock or the ground.
> *In situ:* anything that is already in place and does not need to be placed by the climber.
> **Rack:** all the climbing kit that you carry on your harness.

CHAPTER 13

SELF-RESCUE

For this chapter to be useful you will need to already be a reasonably experienced climber. The skills will be briefly described but cannot be laid out in the same way as building a belay or tying a knot. It would be best to get an idea of these skills from this book and then find an experienced instructor to take you through it at the crag.

When we head out rock climbing, we often go to places that are relatively remote and on to a face of rock where a rescue may be difficult. If you run into trouble it is a good idea to have a few tricks up your sleeve to sort out some basic problems. Remember that the simplest solution to your problem is usually the best. Getting your mate to stand up on a small ledge is far easier than setting up a haul system. Shouting for help and waiting for a helicopter may be safer than attempting a complicated rescue.

The following section will outline a few basic skills rather than tell you what to do in every possible situation. Most of the

Pete Smith and Kat Freeman escaping bad weather on the Lotus Flower Tower.

SELF-RESCUE

problems you will come across will be very simple to fix with a little ingenuity. Should your partner become seriously injured, you must remember that your first priority is *your own safety* – you will be of no use to them if you are injured. The skills below are methods that can be used to get to your casualty in order to give them basic first aid. All of these skills require some practice in order to effect them efficiently. Always take a little time to think and make a plan before starting a rescue.

Rescue Skills

Tying Off Your Belay Device

Most rescues start with the belay plate being tied-off. Once this is done, you will have both hands free and will be able to plan your next step. Later on, however, you will almost undoubtedly wish to regain control of the device, so the tie-off needs to be releasable under load.

Half-Hitch the Dead Rope Tie a half-hitch in the dead rope around the back bar of your belay carabiner. Pass the rope coming out of the belay device through the carabiner to make a small loop of rope on the other side. Then take a bight of dead rope around the outside of the back bar and through this loop. Tighten up the hitch and make sure you leave a good sized loop.

Add Two Full Hitches for Security The half-hitch essentially locks off the live rope but, as it is easily released, we need to put two full hitches around the back bar. Take the large bight of rope in the half-hitch and pass it around the back bar and back through itself. Do this twice. If you cannot fit the hitches around your back bar, you can put them around the live rope above the belay device. You should be able to do this without dropping the climber any distance at all, and always keeping a solid hand on the dead rope. A little practice when top roping is a good way to gain confidence with this skill. To release the tied-off belay plate, simply remove the two full hitches and then pull on the dead rope coming out of the first half-hitch until it pops open and you are back in control.

Tying Off an Italian hitch

If you ever need to attach something heavy (like your unconscious partner) to a belay or anchor, you should use a tied-off

Half-hitch the dead rope 1.

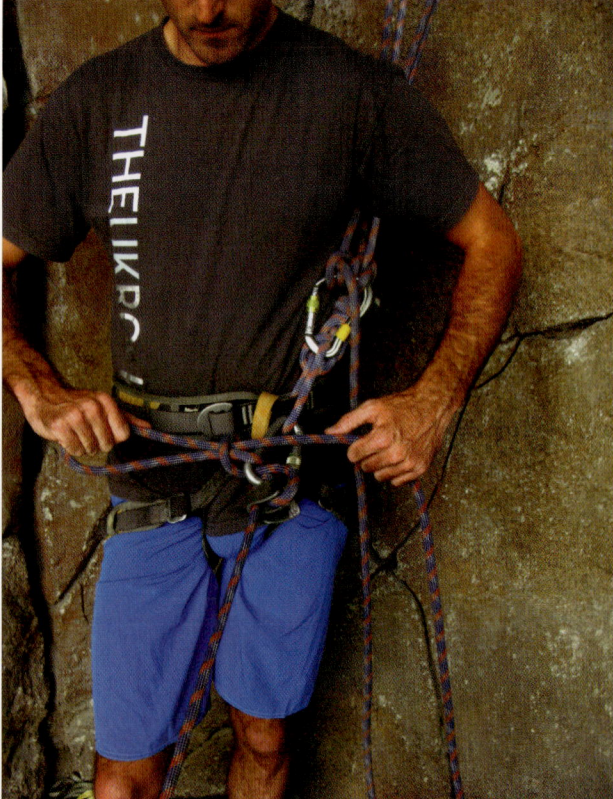

Half-hitch the dead rope 2.

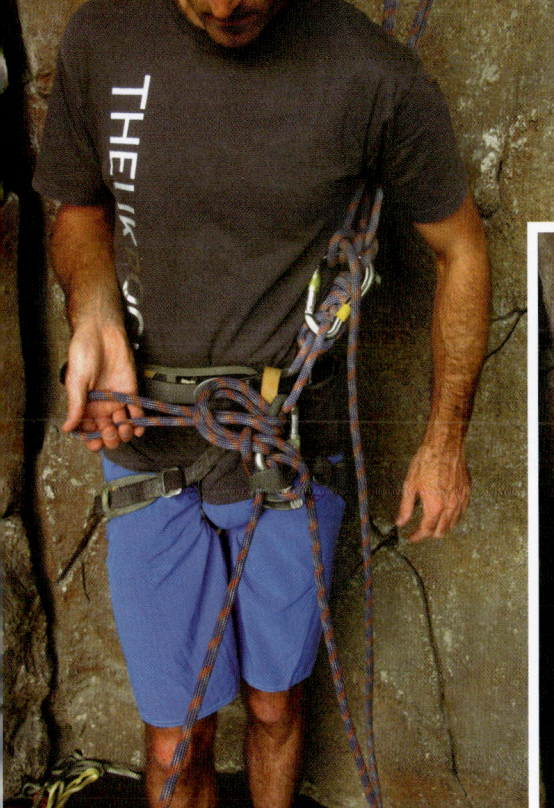

SELF-RESCUE 135

Add a full hitch around the back bar.

BELOW: Add another full hitch around the back bar.

Italian hitch. A tied-off Italian hitch is easily released when loaded. Using it will allow you to release the load onto something else (like the abseil rope) afterwards without any hauling or cutting. You can tie this knot with the rope or a sling, if necessary.

Half-Hitch the Live Rope Hold the dead rope close to the knot, pass some loose dead rope around the back of the live rope and pull a bite of rope through the hole between your hand and the rope. Pull this in tight.

Add Two Full Hitches for Security The half-hitch essentially locks off the live rope but, as it is easily released, we need to put two full hitches around the live rope. This is done by taking the bight of rope made

136 SELF-RESCUE

TOP LEFT: *Half hitch the live rope.*

TOP RIGHT: *Add a full hitch around both ropes.*

BELOW LEFT: *Add another full hitch around both ropes.*

by the half-hitch and passing it around the live rope and the loose dead rope, then pulling the bight back through the gap. Do this twice.

Prusik Knots

There are various ways of tying your prusiks around a rope. Each method has advantages and disadvantages, depending on the situation. Below are three methods that are commonly used.

Traditional Prusik Pass the prusik loop around the rope and through itself three times, as demonstrated in the pictures. This knot is easily loosened when there is no weight on the prusik.

SELF-RESCUE 137

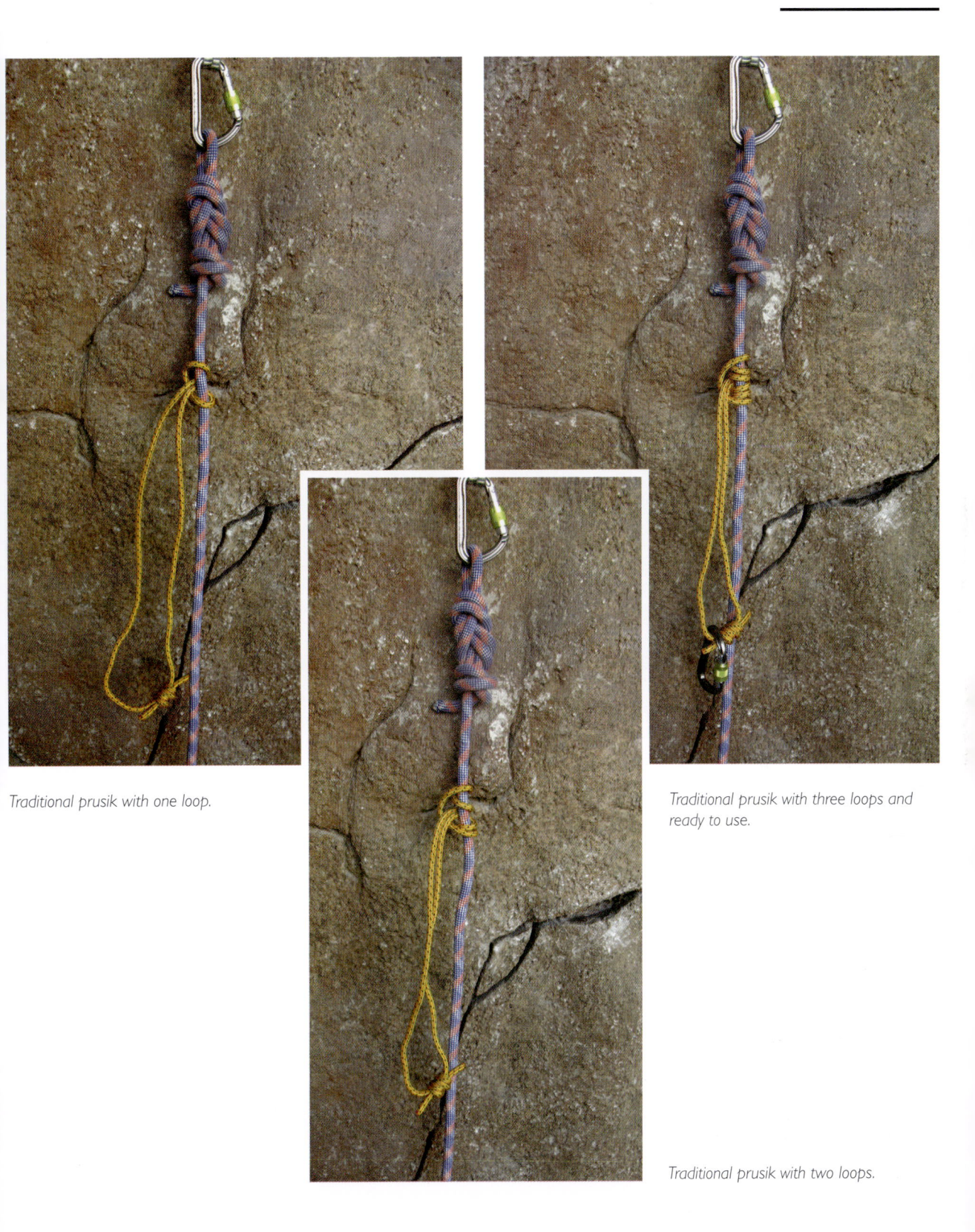

Traditional prusik with one loop.

Traditional prusik with three loops and ready to use.

Traditional prusik with two loops.

SELF-RESCUE

French prusik.

Klemhiest prusik.

French Prusik A French prusik is made by wrapping the prusik cord around the rope and clipping both ends together. It is easily unlocked when loaded but does not bite as hard as the traditional or klemhiest.

Klemhiest Wrap the prusik around the rope but leave a longer tail at the bottom than at the top. Then pass the bottom tail through the top and clip the bottom tail only. This prusik knot bites the rope very hard and can be hard to release when loaded.

Escaping the System

If your climber is incapacitated you may need to leave your belay to go for help, or to go down and give them first aid. If you happen to be belaying directly from your anchors, then you are already out of the system. However, if you are belaying from your harness, then there is a simple manoeuvre you can make to escape the system.

Tie Off the Belay Device See tying off your belay device for details.

Make a Single, Equalized Attachment Point If you are lucky enough to be able to reach back to a sling belay that has a single, equalized attachment point, then you can move straight to the next section (Get a Prusik on the Live Rope). If this is not the case, however, it is easy to make one with a sling:

- Take a sling and wrap it around all the ropes that make up the belay stance.
- Wrap it around as many times as you need to use up the whole length of the sling.
- Leave a tail at the bottom and no tail at the top, then feed the bottom loop through the top loop and tighten it up (as with the klemhiest prusik knot).
- This loop is now your single equalized attachment point.

Get a Prusik on the Live Rope In the example I have used a klemhiest prusik.

Bypass the Belay Device Clip the prusik on the live rope to the single, equalized attachment point and push the prusik down the live rope until it is as tight as you

Wrap a sling around the belay ropes.

140 SELF-RESCUE

Long tail at the bottom, short tail at top.

SELF-RESCUE 141

Bottom tail through the top one to make a klemhiest.

142 SELF-RESCUE

Prusik on the live rope.

SELF-RESCUE 143

LEFT: Bypass the belay device.

INSERT ABOVE: Release the belay device.

144 SELF-RESCUE

can make it. The live rope is now attached directly back to the anchors, you and your belay device have been bypassed.

Release the Belay Device and Backup the Prusik You can now release the tied-off belay device and slowly move all the weight on to the prusik. Once you are sure the prusik is holding, you need to put a little slack behind it and back it up. In this case you could take the rope back to the attachment point and tie-off an Italian hitch. Prusiks cannot be completely trusted, always back them up with a releasable knot.

Improvised Chest Harness

Next time you are hanging in your harness, try completely relaxing. You will find it is extremely uncomfortable. You will invert slightly, the pressure of the harness will cut across your back and, if you completely relax, your tongue will drop to the roof of your mouth, making breathing very difficult. This is the most likely position an unconscious climber will end up in when hanging in their harness. We will look into how to get to them in a moment but it is important to be able to bring them upright to help them breath more easily when you get there.

A sling with a knot in the middle is the simplest way to bring your climber back into a seated position. Simply put the sling around their arms like a rucksack and clip the two loops to the rope loop or belay loop. If they are going to be hanging on the rope for a long time, then clipping them to a prusik on the rope may be better, as it is more upright; but remember that you may wish to get them off this rope so that you can use it later.

Getting to Your Casualty

So, you have escaped the system, what now? You basically have three options for getting to your casualty: a counter-balance abseil; a fixed abseil; or prusiking up or down the rope. Which one you use will depend on the amount of rope you have to play with.

Backup the prusik.

SELF-RESCUE   145

Counter-Balance Abseil

This must only be attempted if the rock quality around you is good and there is little chance of the rope rubbing significantly against the rock. You will see in a moment that the forces involved can make this a hazardous rescue, but in the right circumstances it is very quick and effective. You will need to have escaped the system and have a single, equalized attachment point to work from. You will also need at least half the rope with you so that you can get down to your casualty. To make the examples clear, the rescuer in the photos is not backed up. You should always have a cow's tail available so that you can clip in while performing this and any other rescue.

Escape the System Escape the system as previously described, but keep your belay device attached to the dead rope.

Create the Counter-Balance Bring the rope between the prusik and your belay device up through a carabiner on the equalized attachment point.

Abseil Down Now set up a prusik on the dead rope. Lean back and abseil off, using the weight of the casualty on the other side of the rope to counter-balance your weight.

This is a very quick way of getting to your casualty. Once you are with them, it would be ideal to build an abseil station immediately (after giving first aid). You may wish to abseil down further to find a better place to build a new abseil station. You can do this by clipping the casualty to your belay loop and abseiling as normal. Be warned, however, that the rope then rubs hugely on any rock above you. Keep any further abseiling on a counter-balance system to an absolute minimum.

If your climber is unconscious, make sure you attach them to your new abseil station using a sling with a tied-off Italian hitch. Once you are both attached to the new abseil station, pull the rope down and set up a releasable abseil and abseil down with your casualty attached to your belay loop (or directly to your belay device if you find this more comfortable).

Improvised chest harness from the front.

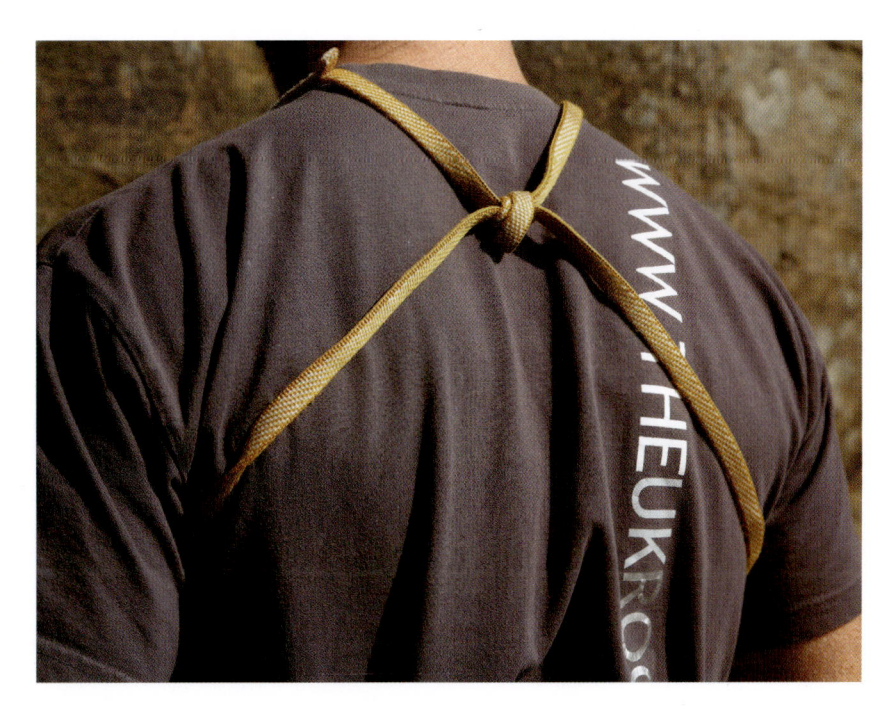

Improvised chest harness from the back.

Escape the system.

SELF-RESCUE 147

Create the counter-balance.

Abseil down.

Snatch Rescue

If you have plenty of rope available you may wish to perform a snatch rescue. This is where you abseil down to the casualty on a separate line, attach them to your harness, detach them from their original line and carry on down, leaving their original rope hanging in space.

Escape the System See escaping the system for details.

Set Up a Fixed Abseil Using all the spare rope available, set up a fixed abseil off the single, equalized attachment point.

Attach Them To Your Line It is best to attach the casualty to the belay device directly with a sling. This keeps their weight on the device, rather than on your harness. The set up shown is a 'Y' hang with one slightly longer side used for the rescuer and the slightly shorter side being attached to the casualty.

Detach Them From the Original Rope If you have a knife, this will be pretty easy (worryingly easy), taut ropes cut very easily. Be careful not to cut towards any other lines or towards your casualty or yourself. Once they are detached from their old line, you can both continue down the crag.

If you do not have a knife then you will need to get the climber's weight off the knot in order to untie it; you can do this with a Yosemite lift. Get a prusik around the rope above the casualty, then put a sling on to their belay loop, up through a carabiner on the prusik and back down to your foot. Stand up on the sling to lift the casualty up a couple of inches. Now undo their knot. This is very strenuous but will work with a bit of effort.

If you can reach the ground with the rope available, then that's great. Otherwise, you will have to attach the casualty to another abseil station (with a sling and a tied-off Italian hitch, if they are unconscious), then prusik back up to retrieve the gear and the rope.

SELF-RESCUE 149

Set up a fixed abseil.

Attach them to your line.

150 SELF-RESCUE

ABOVE: Yosemite lift.

BELOW: Detach them from the original rope.

SELF-RESCUE 151

LEFT: *Attach both prusiks.*

Prusik Knot section). It is made by passing the prusik loop through itself three times around the rope. This prusik is easily unlocked when not loaded, which is why we use it for ascending ropes. Get both prusiks onto the rope, with a screw-gate carabiner on the top one.

Top To Belay Loop and Bottom To Foot Attach the top prusik to your belay loop. Your foot stands in the bottom prusik. If you have slack rope below you, then clove hitch this to a pear-shaped carabiner on your belay loop as a backup knot. If the rope is taut, then you will not be able to use this backup system.

Prusiking

If the casualty is more than half the rope length below you, then prusiking may be the only method of getting to them. It is important to remember that prusik knots can and do slip, so be sure to back them up. If you are on a loose, fixed line, then a backup knot attached to your belay loop is ideal. If, however, you are prusiking down the rope that the casualty is hanging from, you may not have the option of a backup. Sliding prusiks generate a lot of heat and can melt through very quickly. Only move one prusik at a time to avoid any excess heat building up.

Attach Both Prusiks The best prusik to use here is the traditional prusik knot (see

RIGHT: *Top prusik to belay loop, bottom to foot.*

SELF-RESCUE

Ascend or Descend By standing on the bottom prusik, you can unweight the top prusik. Move this top prusik up or down, as necessary, and sit on it. Then move your foot prusik up or down, as necessary, and stand up to unweight the top prusik again. Continue until you arrive at your destination.

Rescuing an Injured Leader

Remember that your own safety is the first priority; without you the casualty has virtually no hope of getting help. If your injured fallen leader is conscious, then you may be able to lower them back to your belay stance. Lowering an unconscious person, however, is generally not a good idea, as they may well get caught on the rock or you may worsen their injuries. If they are hanging in free space, then lowering may be the quickest and safest method of getting them to you. The rescuer will have to make this judgment. Personally, I would only go up to my climber if I thought their airway was compromised or if they were bleeding heavily, and I thought it was safe to do so.

If you decide to go to a fallen leader, you will need to adjust your belay to take an upward pull. Also, you need to be confident that the gear they are hanging on is solid. The major issue with rescuing someone who is above you, is that you will not have personally inspected the gear that you will both end up hanging from. Always look for other options before taking this risk.

So, you have exhausted all other options, you have adjusted your belay to take an upward pull, you have tied-off their rope and are confident in the gear holding the casualty. You can now prusik up the live rope. Once you have reached the climber, you can continue the rescue as the situation dictates, but do not rush. If help is on the way, it may be best just to sit and wait for it to arrive.

Rescuing a fallen leader is probably as complicated as rescues get and should only be attempted if you are sure you can do it safely.

Haul Systems

On occasion you may find that hauling your partner up a route is necessary. Hauling up a heavy load over a long distance on your own is very strenuous. We don't really carry the best kit for hauling as part of our everyday rack. In Yosemite, where many people will haul up massive loads of food, water and bedding, they use static ropes and mechanical pulley systems to make the process easier. Hauling with dynamic rope and prusiks is much harder but still possible. If your climber is conscious and uninjured, it may be much easier for them to prusik up the rope than for you to haul them up.

Ascend or descend.

SELF-RESCUE 153

Prusik on the live rope.

Assisted Hoist

If you have a conscious climber and two-thirds of the rope available, then your partner can help with the following system.

Lock Off the Belay Plate See tying off your belay device for details.

Prusik on the Live Rope Get a prusik on the live rope. Wrap it around three or four times and clip both ends together (a French prusik) and clip this back to your belay device's carabiner. This turns your belay device into a semi-auto-locking device.

Lower a Loop of Dead Rope The dead rope is lowered down to the climber. They clip this loop of rope to their belay loop. The rope now runs from the climber's knot, up through your now semi-auto-locking belay device, down through a carabiner on the climber's belay loop and back up to your hands.

Both Start Pulling You can now pull on the rope in your hands and your partner can pull on the rope coming from your belay device. The climber will start to come up the route quickly and easily.

Lower a loop of dead rope.

154 SELF-RESCUE

Both start pulling.

Belay device onto single equalized attachment point, with a prusik for assisted breaking.

Clip the dead rope.

Unassisted Hoist

This is a three-way pulley system set up next to the belay. It is the same as the last system except that it works from a prusik on the live rope, rather than from the climber's belay loop. Unassisted hoists are very hard to effect from within the system. It is best to escape the system and set it up directly from the belay. Getting some assistance pulling will make a huge difference. If I had to haul someone to the top of a crag, I would find as many people as possible to help.

Escape the System See escaping the system for details.

Belay Device on to Single, Equalized Attachment Point Attach the belay device to your single, equalized attachment point. Back it up with a prusik on the live rope, just in front of the belay plate, clipped back to the belay device's carabiner.

Clip the Dead Rope The dead rope coming out of the belay plate is now clipped through a carabiner that is attached to a

SELF-RESCUE 155

Abseil down close to the knot.

Prusik on the live rope.

second prusik on the live rope. You now have a three-to-one pulley system, with the rope running from your semi-auto-locking belay device, through the lower prusik and back to your hands. Three-to-one means that for every 30cm you pull up, the climber will move up 10cm.

Start Pulling As you pull, the second prusik will move up towards the belay plate, dragging the climber up the route. Once you cannot pull it any further up, gently release the load until the semi-auto-locking belay device takes hold and then move the second prusik back down the live rope. Repeat.

Passing a Knot

Abseiling Past a Knot

There are a couple of reasons you may wish to abseil past a knot. One is that your rope has been damaged and you have isolated the damaged section by tying an overhand knot in the rope, so that the damaged section is in the loop and not the main body of the rope. Another reason would be to abseil further than you can with one rope in one go. If you tie two 60m ropes together, then you can abseil 120m in one fixed abseil. This could get you out of trouble fast if someone was injured or the weather made a turn for the worse. However, you would need to pass the knot in the middle safely.

Abseil Down Close to the Knot You will need to keep some distance between yourself and the knot at all times. Getting the knot jammed into your belay device would be a bad move, as you would need to move back up to release yourself. Abseil down until the knot is within reach.

Prusik on Live Rope Get a prusik on the rope above your belay device and attach yourself to it. I recommend a sling with a tied-off Italian hitch for this job, in case you struggle to release the prusik knot; but this is not necessarily essential.

156 SELF-RESCUE

Move belay device below the knot.

Backup the prusik.

SELF-RESCUE 157

Remove the prusik and back up.

158 SELF-RESCUE

ABOVE: Prep the anchors.

BELOW: Lower until close to the knot.

Backup the Prusik Take the rope below the knot and clove hitch it to your belay loop. This is the backup to the top prusik, should it slip or fail.

Move the Belay Device Below the Knot Now you are hanging off the top prusik and backed up below, you can remove your belay device and abseiling prusik and re-attach them below the knot

Remove the Prusik and Backup Remove the backup clove hitch and replace it with a couple of turns around your leg. Now slide the top prusik down until the weight comes onto your belay device. You should now be free to abseil down the rest of the rope.

Lowering Past a Knot

You can lower someone past a knot using a similar method. Preparation is the key to this working well.

Prepare the Anchors Before starting to lower, get everything ready on the single, equalized attachment point. You will need an Italian hitch on the live rope ready to lower your partner. Have a sling with a prusik attached to the same point but hanging free. The rope behind the knot you wish to pass is attached to the same point with a tied-off Italian hitch (in this example it is attached to the second set of anchors so as to give a clear demonstration).

Lower Until Close to the Knot Make sure you leave some room before you get to the knot. Then tie-off the first Italian hitch.

Prusik on the Live Rope Get a prusik on the taut live rope in front of the tied-off Italian hitch and clipped back to the attachment point. Push it down the rope until it is as tight as you can get it.

Remove the First Italian Hitch Get rid of the first Italian hitch and slowly release the prusik until all the weight comes onto the second Italian hitch. Be sure not to let the knot touch the prusik or you will not be able to release it.

Remove the Prusik Once the prusik is removed, you can release the second Italian hitch and continue to lower.

SELF-RESCUE

SELF-RESCUE: IN SHORT

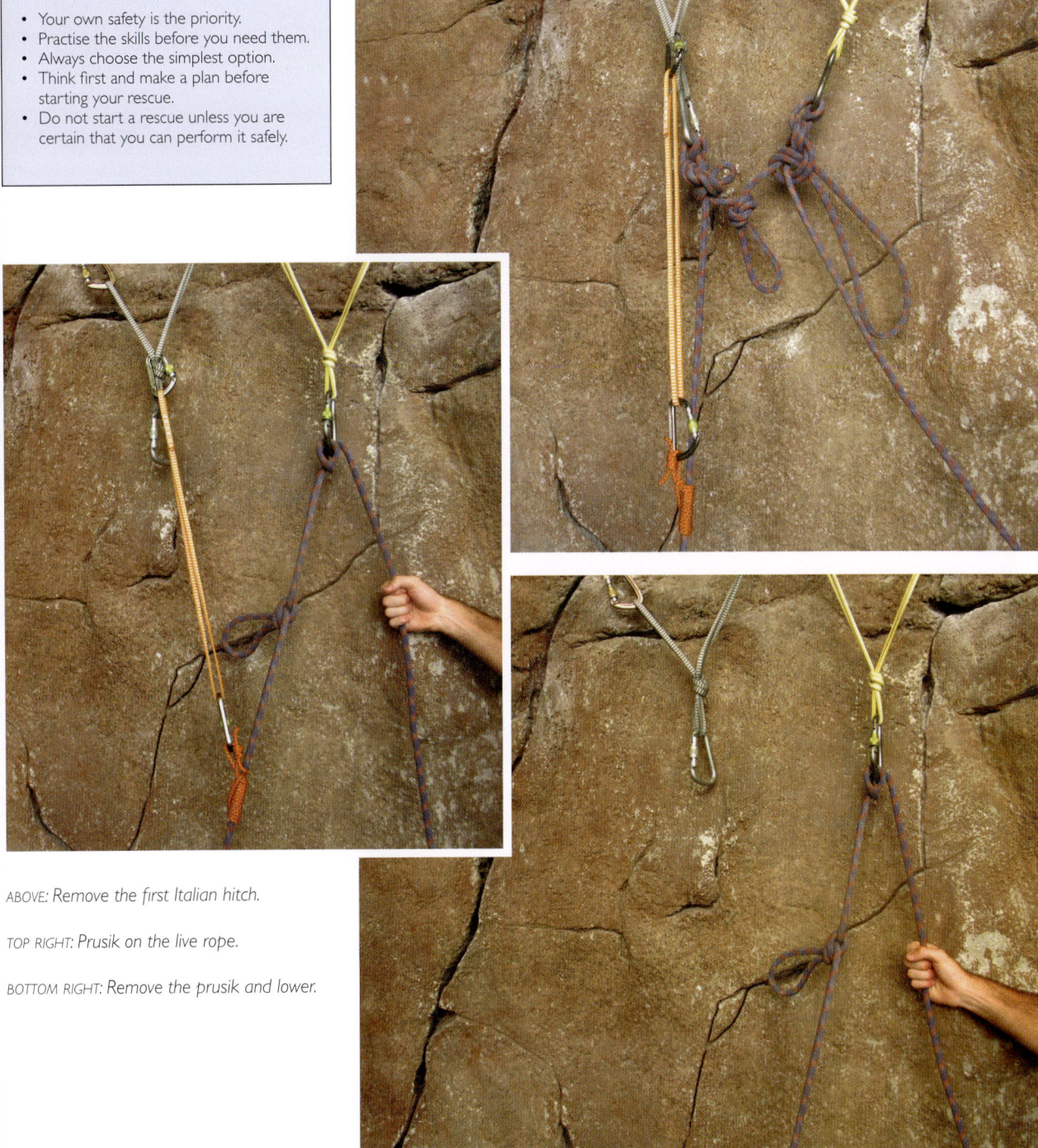

- Your own safety is the priority.
- Practise the skills before you need them.
- Always choose the simplest option.
- Think first and make a plan before starting your rescue.
- Do not start a rescue unless you are certain that you can perform it safely.

ABOVE: *Remove the first Italian hitch.*

TOP RIGHT: *Prusik on the live rope.*

BOTTOM RIGHT: *Remove the prusik and lower.*

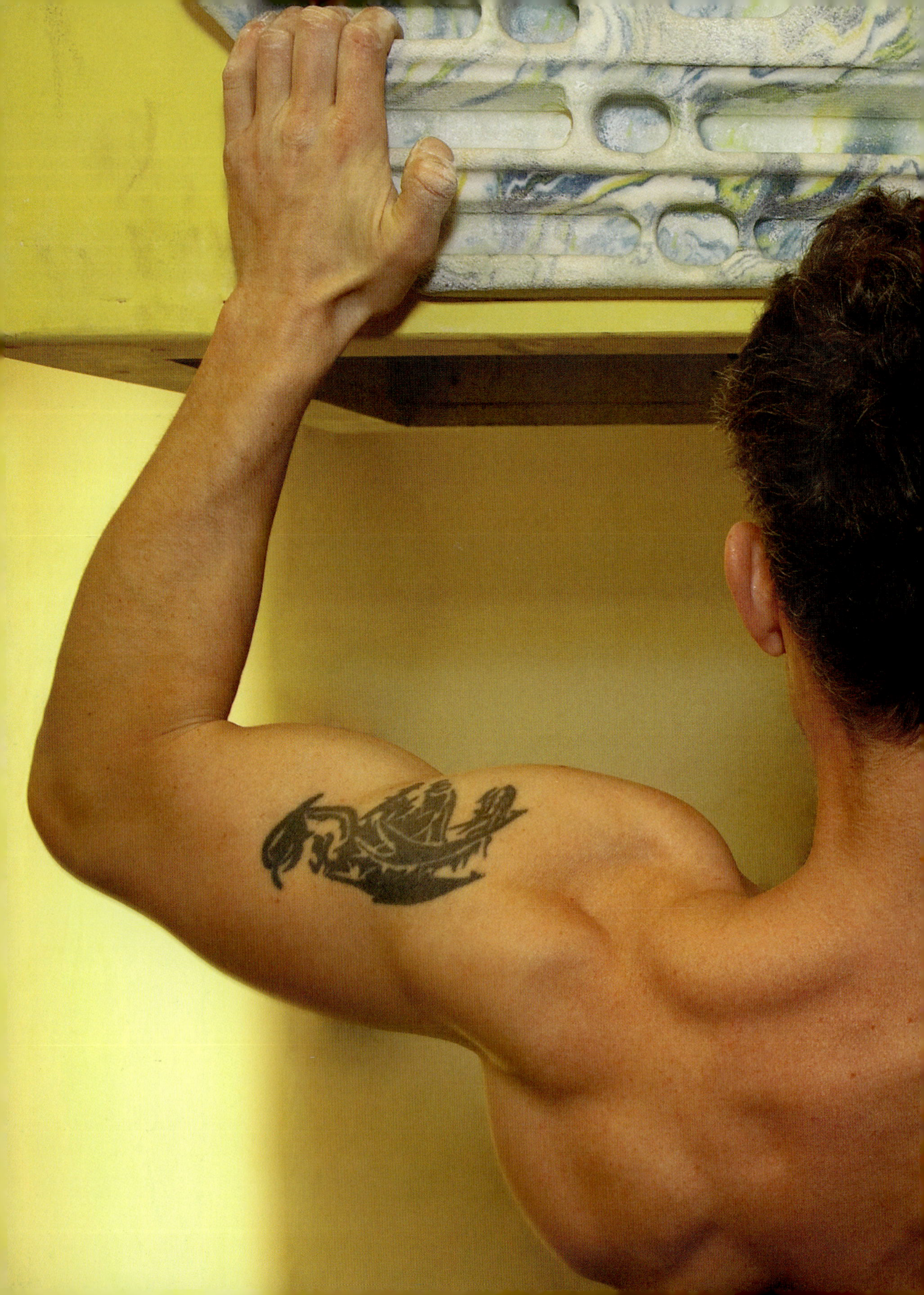

PART 3
CLIMBING TECHNIQUE AND TRAINING

CHAPTER 14

TECHNIQUES

Climbing performance can be spilt into three equal parts: one part physical, one part mental and one part technical.

I will not try to go through all the techniques needed for every possible situation. Below is just a basic outline of some principles that you should try to develop.

Precise Footwork

The key to good footwork is precision and confidence. There are two basic foot placements that every beginner should be aware of: edging and smearing.

Edging is used when you have a flat edge to stand on. Make sure you use the sides of your feet near your toes and get the edge of your shoe really snug up against the wall. In both the examples provided, you will see the heel is away from the wall so as to bring the inside or outside edge parallel to the rock.

Smearing is used when there is no positive edge to stand on. Bringing your heels down and out puts pressure into the wall and builds up friction between your shoe and the rock. Always look out for small changes in the angle of the rock, just a small decrease in angle will make smearing much easier.

Jamming

When face-climbing you will use a variety of different types of holds for your hands at a variety of angles. Slopers, crimps, pockets, jugs and pinches are some of the types of holds you will come across, and you will end up using them, however they present themselves to you.

Inside edging.

Outside edging.

TECHNIQUES 163

ABOVE: *Smearing.*

TOP RIGHT: *Fist jam, fingers extended.*

RIGHT: *Fist jam, fingers into the palm.*

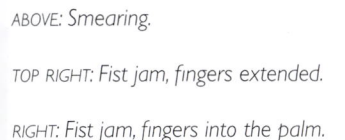

However, when you start crack climbing it can be a bit baffling, at first. With nothing to pull on directly, you will have to jam your fingers, hands or fists (depending on the size of the crack) into the crack, so that you are pressing out on both sides equally. Once you are jammed in, then you can move on.

With fist jamming, you put your hand in, straight on, with your palm towards the crack and then make a fist. Your hand is wider in a fist than when flat and this expansion locks your fist in place.

To hand jam, place your hand into the crack vertically and flat. Now bring your thumb into the middle of your palm and press your finger tips against the rock. Again, this makes your hand wider and should wedge it into the crack.

For small cracks, place your fingers into the crack side on, then twist your hand down so that your fingers stack on top of one another. This twisting action locks your finger in place.

Your feet may well have to jam in the crack as well. This is done by placing your foot into the crack side on, then twisting it back towards its neutral position. Foot jams can be painful in super tight technical shoes, so choose your footwear carefully if you are heading to a crack climbing venue.

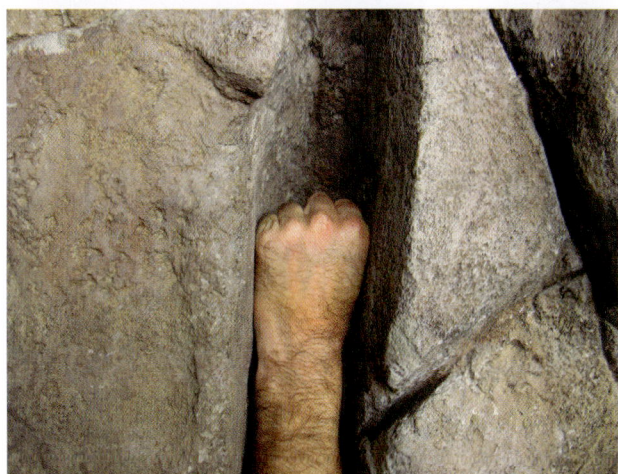

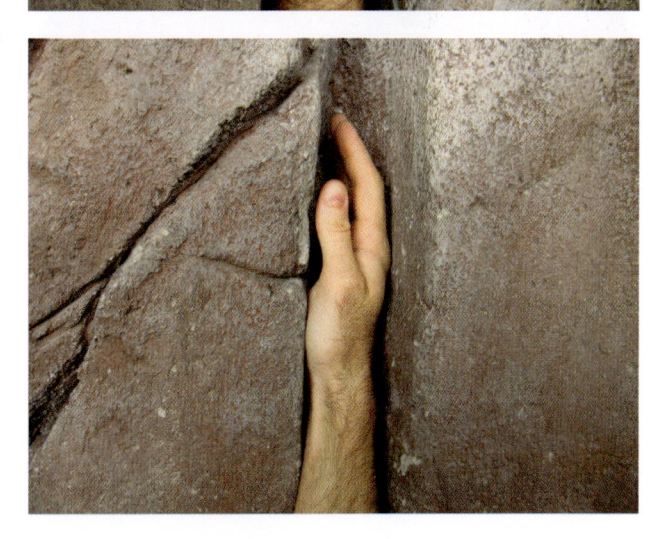

Hand jam, hand placed in the crack.

164 TECHNIQUES

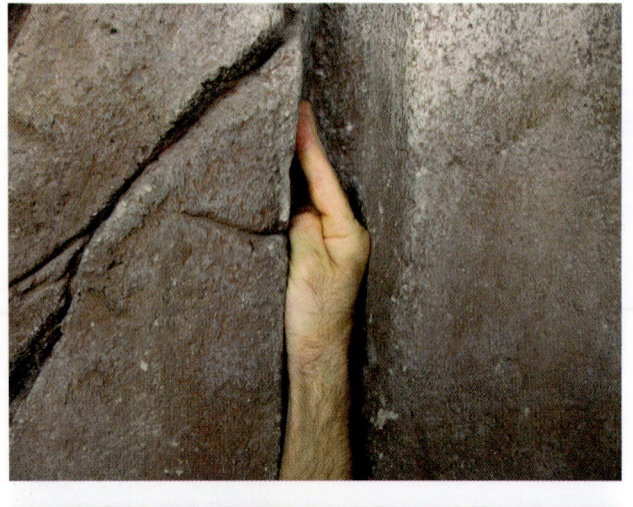

TOP LEFT: Hand jam, fingers pressed on one side and the back of the hand pressed against the other side.

TOP RIGHT: Finger jam, fingers stacked in the crack.

MIDDLE LEFT: Finger jam, hand twisted down to lock fingers in place.

MIDDLE RIGHT: Foot jam, foot placed sideways in a crack.

BOTTOM LEFT: Foot jam, foot twisted back to lock it into the crack.

Balance

Your legs are much stronger than your arms, and are much more capable of holding your weight for long periods of time. It is therefore desirable to keep your centre of gravity over and between your feet, just as this is desirable when standing on the ground so that you do not fall over. On the wall, however, you can counteract an unbalanced position by over-gripping with your hands. Keeping your hips close to the wall will limit the weight taken by your hands and forearms, making your forearm strength last longer. Keeping your handholds between your feet will keep your position balanced preventing you from swinging around out of control. It is worth remembering that poor footholds in the right place are better than good ones that put you out of balance.

BELOW LEFT: GOOD balance, hips close and between the feet.

TOP RIGHT: BAD balance, hips far from the wall puts weight onto the hands.

BELOW RIGHT: BAD balance, hands outside the feet makes the climber unbalanced.

Techniques

Gaining Height

You can use one of three parts of your body to gain height: legs, torso or arms. Using your arms the majority of the time is very inefficient, simply because they are the smallest of the three options.

On slabby or vertical terrain, a rock-over can make full use of your legs to gain height. The principle is that if you have a high foothold, you should be able to transfer your weight over this foot and then stand up using your strong leg muscles. If this is done in a dynamic way, the movement is efficient and requires very little help from your arms. This is more than just an isolated move but is a foundation of good climbing movement.

ABOVE: Rock over, start position.

LEFT: Rock over, weight is thrown over the bent leg.

TECHNIQUES 167

Rock over, the leg then pushes the body up towards the next hand hold.

TECHNIQUES

On overhanging terrain, twisting can bring your torso and legs together to enable you to gain height without pulling on your arms. If you want to bring your right hand up, then turn your right foot onto its outside edge. Now, maintaining a straight left arm, push with your left leg and twist your torso to face left, while your right hand reaches to the next hold.

TECHNIQUES 169

JARGON

Crimp: a small positive edge held with the pads of your finger tips.
Face climbing: climbing a vertical, sparsely featured wall.
Jug: a good positive hold.
Pinch: a hold that requires you to squeeze with your thumb.
Pocket: a hole in the rock.
Slab (slabby): an easy angled area of rock that leans away from you.
Sloper: a hand hold with no positive edge.

ABOVE: *Drop knee, right knee drops.*

RIGHT: *Drop knee, left leg pushes you towards the next hold, arms stay straight.*

OPPOSITE PAGE: *Drop knee, start position.*

CHAPTER 15

TECHNIQUE TRAINING

Most people do not really understand how to train their technique. In a way, it is a natural process of trial and error. When you don't get up a problem, the technique must have been poor but when you do get up the problem, the technique worked. However, this form of technique training will only get you so far, eventually you will plateau. The following are some games that you can play during your session to improve your technique.

Warm Up/Drills

No-one does drills, right? In every other sport, from tennis to gymnastics, drills are used to improve technique, so why isn't it done in climbing? Every time you warm up you have an opportunity to hone a few techniques. If you do this every session, let's say twice a week, that is at least a hundred times a year. See the warm-up section below for some ideas but essentially choose a technique that you want to work on and climb an easy route focusing on this technique alone. Keep it as part of your warm up until you feel comfortable with the skill and then move on to another.

Eliminator

This is a simple game that helps you create your own boulder problems. Start with a boulder wall or face that is covered in holds. Climb from one point to another using all the holds, then remove one (one that you used!) and do it again. Keep going until you are climbing the wall with the smallest number of holds possible. You can play this on your own or with a few mates. The best thing about this game is that you will be forced to do moves that you are not used to trying.

Chunking

Most hard routes are just a string of easier routes stacked on top of each other. When tackling a boulder problem or a route that is beyond your current level, it can be daunting. Let's say you want to climb a relatively long (ten move) V4 but have only ever climbed V3. A long V4 is often just two short V3s stacked one on top of the other. Work your route in sections, try to overlap these chunks and get each section completely wired, so that when you come to attempt the full problem you are being totally efficient throughout.

Cheat to Win

Let's say you come across a stopper move on your project at the local wall. The whole move requires you to throw your left hand from an edge by your hip to a pocket way over the top of your sloping, right handhold. The whole move may feel daunting and well beyond your current level, but you need to get on this grade to learn how to climb it. In a climbing wall you will normally have a few extra holds around to help you, use these holds as intermediates within the move.

So, set yourself up for the move, then throw your left hand over but latch a few holds on the way to your final destination. Your right hand and your feet *must* stay on their original holds. Only your left hand cheats on its way through the move. This cheating teaches you the individual body positions you will need to go through to complete the move. As these positions get easier, reduce the number of intermediates until you are completing the move without cheating.

Add-Ons

Everyone has strengths and weaknesses. This game highlights strengths and weaknesses in your own and your friends' technique, and forces you to attempt moves out of your comfort zone.

Stand at the bottom of a bouldering wall with some mates. Choose a starting hold, hang onto it and make one move to any other hold, then come off the wall. Now your mate gets on the starting hold, moves to the same hold you chose and then adds another hold. Repeat this process until you get to a natural finishing move. The problem created will be a merge of each player's style. It is best to stipulate that no swapping hands is allowed, and remember that a bit of healthy competition is good, so throw in a couple of moves you know your partner hates…

Memory Game

Being able to memorize sequences of moves is a massive advantage when climbing at your limit. When you hit a poor hold in the middle of your project, two seconds looking around for the next hold could cost you dearly. Try playing the previous game (add-ons) but do not allow anyone to mark up any of the holds or tell the climber where the next hold is while they are climbing. If you get it wrong, then you miss your go.

Many people think they cannot memorize routes because they have a bad memory. I have a terrible memory for important things (birthdays, shopping lists, conversations) but can memorize a fifty-move sequence in a few minutes. The reason is that I practise memorizing sequences (instead of important dates).

Memory works by association. Look at every hold you are about to use and give it a descriptive name (pocket, cheese block, nose, whatever it looks like to you), and build up a sequence of associated shapes in your head. Practise while your mate climbs by mimicking their movements while saying the name of each hold in turn. With a little practice, your memory for sequences will be as honed as your ability to remember where you keep the food in your kitchen.

CHAPTER 16

MENTAL TRAINING

Mental training should be seen as an everyday exercise that can be done at the crag, but also whenever you have ten minutes free to think. Mental training is often neglected and I know plenty of extremely strong climbers that are dragging a massive (metaphorical) weight up every climb they do. The following are just a few examples of mental tactics to improve your game.

Be Positive – Always!

A positive attitude will help you climb harder. Whenever you fall off a route or problem, there is always a positive to be taken from it, such as 'that was good fall practice,' or 'I fell off because my foot slipped, next time I will place it more carefully,' or any other lesson you can gain from the experience.

Climb With Positive People

Negativity breeds negativity – avoid negative people. You want a climbing partner who wants to be there, who wants to climb well, who wants you to climb well, who wants to climb hard and have fun. Most importantly, you want to be that climbing partner for someone else.

Have a Goal

Any goal will do, so long as it pushes you beyond your current level. It is much easier to fight on through the lactic acid burn when there is a tangible reward waiting for you at the end. Your goal may be a specific route or a grade or to be champion of the world, anything will do so long as it is realistically achievable within a given time-frame. Remind yourself of this goal during your session to boost your focus.

Face Your Fears

Think about it really carefully. What is your true fear? What is the fear that gets in the way of your goals? Usually it is fear of falling or fear of failure that gets in the way. So long as there isn't any real danger, then these fears are easy to get over by exposing yourself to them on a regular basis. If you find falling difficult, then start falling off all the time (see Chapter 9). If fear of failure is the problem, then get on routes that you will fail on every session. Eventually any fear can be reversed but it will require work and the work needs to start now.

Make Your Weakness Your Strength

It is so easy to get into the habit of going to the wall or crag and doing the same routes you have done a hundred times before. These routes feel secure mentally and physically, and therefore do not challenge you enough to teach you anything new. If you always do the same thing, don't be surprised when you get the same result.

So, if you hate overhangs, get on them every session until you love them. If you hate pinches, find the pinchiest route you can and get on it. If you hate cracks, then get on every pure crack climb you can find. Weaknesses are simply a product of inexperience of that particular terrain or technique. Get the experience and it will become another one of your strengths.

Visualize

A study of basketball players in Australia holds some great value to all sports people. They split a team up and for twenty days got one half to practice free throws physically, while the other half simply visualized the same practice. At the end of the experiment both halves had improved by pretty much the same amount (physical practice 24 per cent, mental practice 23 per cent improvement).

With climbing you can only train so many times a week, but you can visualize your goals everyday. Memorize your projects, move for move, and then walk through them, in your mind, when you are at home relaxing. Remember that if you find it hard in your mind, it will be hard in body, so when you visualize make sure you are smiling, the holds feel bomber and that every move is graceful.

CHAPTER 17

PHYSICAL TRAINING

Technique and mental training should be a constant feature in your climbing sessions. However, if you want to climb like a pro, some dedicated physical training will eventually be necessary. There are basically three types of training that you can focus on: power, power endurance and endurance, all of which should start with a warm up and finish with a warm down.

Power training is all about recruitment – training your muscles to fire more of the fibres they already have, rather than making them bigger. Big muscles are heavy, which means you have to drag more weight up the wall. Small, powerful muscles are much more efficient for climbers.

Power endurance training makes your muscles more resistant to the effects of lactic acid (or being pumped). With good power endurance you can still pull moves near your limit, even though you are pumped out of your mind.

Endurance training should help you recover while on routes. With good endurance training you will find that you can shake out and recover your muscles mid-route. To start with, you may need a massive jug and great feet but eventually you will need less and less in order to shake out and get back some power.

Warm Up

There is not much that is more boring or embarrassing than doing star jumps in front of a busy bouldering wall. However, there is nothing more damaging and detrimental to your body and climbing performance than getting straight on to hard grades as soon as you turn up. This warm-up is designed to be fun and to prepare your body and (just as importantly) your mind, for the activity you are about to perform.

Pulse Raiser

This is probably the most overlooked section of a good warm-up. The idea is to get blood deep into your muscles and loosen up your body ready for the strains you are going to put on it.

Three to five minutes of jogging (on the spot or en route to the crag), while clenching and flexing your hands, should do the trick.

Climbing Reps

The following reps are designed to get your mind and body in tune with one another and are also a good way to work on specific weaknesses. These are some examples of common weaknesses, but if you struggle with something else (swapping feet, for example), then add that in.

Indoor walls will normally have a traverse wall, which is a good place for these reps. However, at the crag you may be able to find an area at the base to climb around on, or you can use an easy route and take turns with your partner. Do a complete traverse or a short route for each of the following exercises.

Focus Slow, precise climbing, watching every hand and foot placement. Forgetting about the stresses of work and life in general. This can also be a good time to practise positive thought. Give yourself a mantra (e.g. I am strong, I am light, I am technical, I love my life, I can climb 7a) and repeat it as you climb.

Feet Concentrate on precise, quiet foot placement. Watch your feet all the way on to each hold. Your feet are the key to good climbing.

Fluid Try to make every move flow into the next. Keep quiet feet. This tunes your body into moving efficiently.

Fast Keep quiet feet and fluid motion but speed it up. When climbing on steep terrain with no available rests, the best tactic is to move fast (so long as you do not lose form).

Start Climbing You are not quite ready to climb at your limit just yet. Make sure you work up through the grades, rather than jumping on your project straight after the warm-up.

Power

Power training is done on problems of six to ten moves long. The idea is *not* to get pumped but to have quality attempts at problems. For this reason, it is essential to have a 30 – 60s rest per move completed. So, if you complete six moves, you need to take a minimum of three minutes rest before getting back on the wall.

Warm Up

See Warm Up section.

Warm Up Extended

Do problems on all terrains (slab, vertical and over hanging), progressing through the grades. You are now ready to train.

Training

- Choose two problems that will take you about ten attempts to achieve. It is

best to work them in short sections and try to link these sections together.
- You should *not* be getting pumped.
- Remember, 30 – 60s rest per move completed!

Warm Down

Once you feel you cannot pull near your limit any more. Start to regress back through the grades until well within your ability. See Warm Down section for more details.

Stretch

See Stretching section for details.

Power Endurance

During each power endurance set, you should keep moving from hold to hold with no pause in your movement. When you fall off, it should be from muscle failure, rather than because you feel tired. If you are hanging around on big jugs shaking out, then you are moving into pure endurance training, which is a different form of training and will be less helpful when you need to pull consistently hard moves.

Warm Up

See Warm Up section.

Training

- Choose a route a whole grade lower than what you regularly on-sight (for example, 6a if you regularly on-sight 6b) and climb six routes at this grade with limited rest in-between each route. If you do not have a partner, you can make up a circuit (circular boulder problem) of approximately thirty moves.
- Rest time should be equal to the time spent on the wall. So if it takes two minutes to climb the wall, take two minutes rest between each route.
- You should be failing on the last couple of attempts. If you complete them, then do more reps or increase the grade. If you fail very quickly, then decrease the grade.

Warm Down

See Warm Down section.

Endurance

During this type of training you are trying to get better at resting mid-route. Feel free to stop and shake out from any good hold but avoid using bridges or anything else that takes the majority of the weight off your arms.

Warm Up

See Warm Up section.

Warm Up Extended

Work up through the grades until you are near your on-sight grade.

Training

- During this session you will climb up, down and back up a route so that you triple the amount of climbing you do in one push. The route you climb up should be one full grade lower than your current on-sight grade. So if you on-sight 6b, then drop down to 6a.
- If you are training at an indoor lead climbing wall, the ideal line for a 6b climber would have a 6a and a 5+ route on it. Climb up the 6a, down the 5+ and back up the 6a.
- If you are lucky enough to be able to get to a crag regularly and want to train endurance there, you can simply climb up, down and up a 6a. If you struggle with the climb down, you can cheat a little by grabbing a quickdraw, but try to avoid hanging on the rope.
- If your climbing wall does not have suitable routes or you do not have a partner, then make up a circuit with thirty to fifty moves and do it three times.
- When you have completed one set, take a good rest (at least fifteen minutes) and then repeat, preferably on a different route. Do as many sets as time and energy allows.

Warm Down

See Warm Down section.

Warm Down

Warming down is important for your body and climbing performance. When you climb or do any physical exercise, your muscles deteriorate. When you rest in-between sessions, they grow back bigger and/or stronger. Warming down primes them for this process by clearing out impurities, like lactic acid. Stretching lengthens and increases the flexibility of the muscles, and prevents scar tissue from forming.

Warm-Down Climbs

Once you have finished training or passed your peak, bring the grade down one by one until you are climbing something super easy.

Antagonist Muscles

Climbing is often described as a full body workout. In a sense this is true, but it definitely works some muscles more than others. The front of your forearms, for instance, get massively worked during climbing, whereas the back of your forearms do comparatively little.

PHYSICAL TRAINING 175

This imbalance can create classic overuse injuries. Typically, climbers get problems with elbows and shoulders (rotator cuffs). A few simple exercises after every session can help prevent these problems.

It is a good idea to invest in a Thera-band of some sort, as they are extremely useful for performing antagonistic exercises. They can be bought at most good sports or gym equipment stores or online.

Reverse Wrist Curls

These train the back of your forearms and helps to avoid common elbow injuries. Place a Thera-band under your feet and hold the ends in your hands. Have your elbows at 90 degrees, close to your body and allow your wrists to hang low. Now bring your wrists up and slowly back down until the back of your forearm is burning. You should compete three sets every session.

TOP LEFT: *Wrists are down, elbows at 90 degrees.*

TOP RIGHT: *Bring wrists up slowly.*

BELOW: *Bring wrists all the way up and then slowly back down.*

Rotator Cuff

Tie one end of your Thera-band to something solid at about elbow height (a door handle works well), put a rolled up T-shirt or towel between your elbow and your chest, have your elbow locked at 90 degrees while holding onto the tensioned Thera-band. Now, only using the muscles in your shoulder and behind your scapular, bring your hand out to around 45 degrees from your body. Repeat until the front of your shoulder is burning. Three sets every session.

Press-ups

In climbing you train your pulling arm muscles much more than your pushing arm muscles. It is a good idea, therefore, to do a few sets of press-ups at the end of your session to balance out your training.

You want to do three sets of about 70 per cent of your current best. So, if you can do ten press-ups, then do three sets

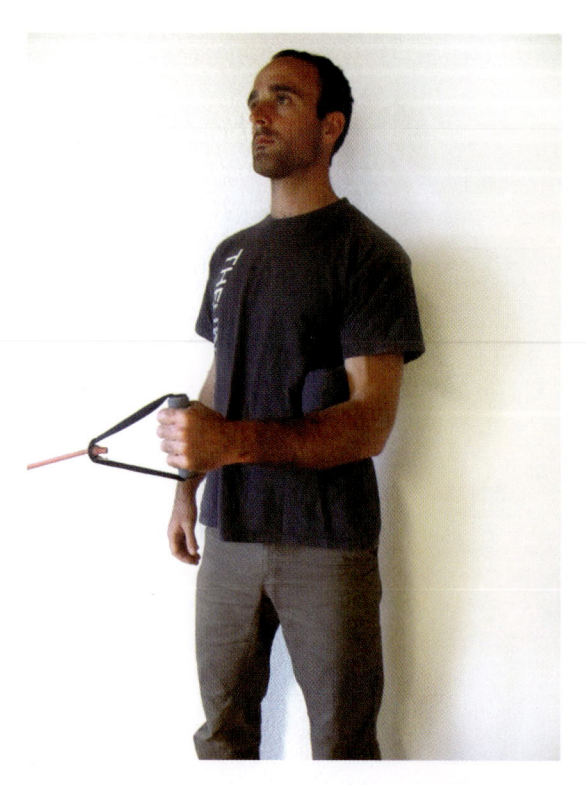

LEFT: *Elbow at 90 degrees, tension on the Thera-band.*

BELOW LEFT: *Bring elbow out away from the body.*

BELOW RIGHT: *Come out to 45 degrees and then back to original position.*

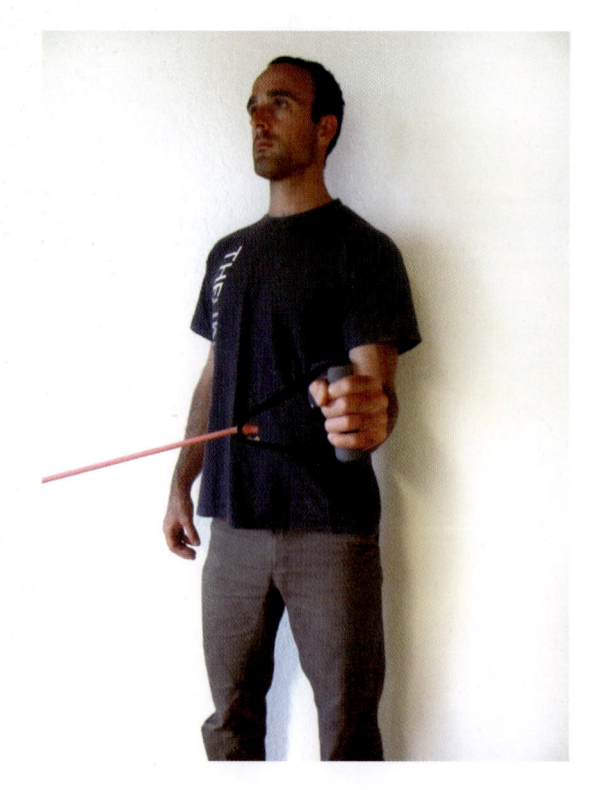

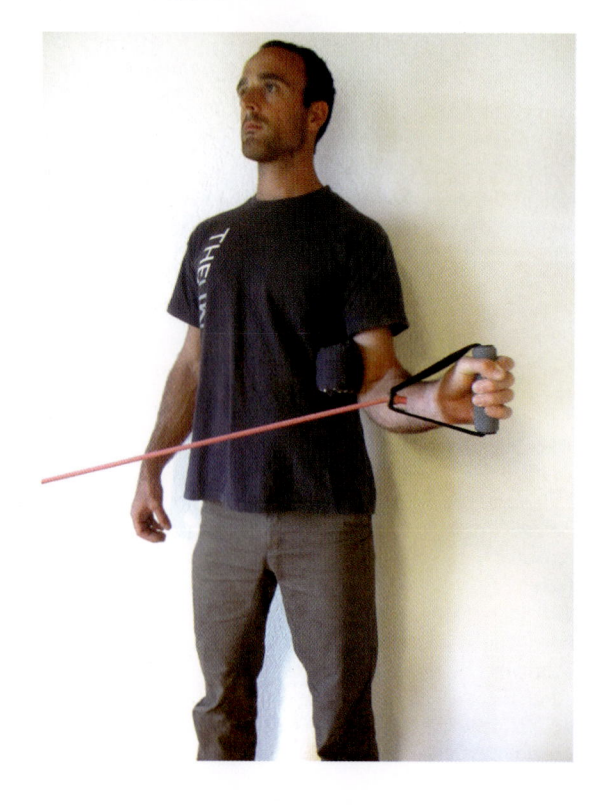

of seven; if you can do twenty, then do three sets of fourteen.

Stretching

The end of your session is a good time to stretch your muscles, as they are warm and malleable. Work through your body from top to bottom stretching all the major muscle groups. All stretches should be slowly pushed into until felt, then all movement should stop. Hold each stretch for about thirty seconds.

Stretches should not be painful! You cannot get quick results from stretching.

Forearms Front and Back

Your forearms take the brunt of the abuse in climbing, so it is especially important to stretch them out to avoid injury. Make sure you stretch both sides. To stretch the front of your forearms, kneel down and place both palms flat on the floor with your fingers pointing behind you. Now lean back until you feel a stretch through the muscle.

To stretch the back of your forearms, do the same but with the back of your hands on the floor. You should feel a stretch from the back of your hand to your elbow.

Biceps and Triceps

To stretch your biceps, place the back of your hand against a flat wall, then turn your body 90 degrees to the wall and step forward with the foot closest to the wall.

Your triceps are stretched by bringing your hand up and over your head, and then reaching down your spine. The other hand can help push it further, to deepen the stretch.

Neck

Your neck can take a lot of strain while climbing and also when belaying, as you

Stretch, forearms front.

Stretch, forearms back.

178 PHYSICAL TRAINING

Stretch, triceps.

Stretch, biceps.

PHYSICAL TRAINING

tend to look up all the time. Stand in a neutral position, then drop your left ear to your left shoulder. Imagine you have a heavy weight in your right hand to get a stretch up into the right side of your neck stemming from your shoulder.

Shoulders and Chest

Start in a neutral standing position, then bring your right arm across your body and hold it next to your left shoulder with your left hand. This lengthens the muscles around your right shoulder.

To stretch your chest muscles, stand next to a wall. Place the forearm of your right arm against the wall with your elbow at 90 degrees and your fingers pointing to the sky. Then bring your weight forward by stepping your right foot past the wall into a lunge position.

ABOVE: *Stretch, neck.*

RIGHT: *Stretch, shoulder.*

180 PHYSICAL TRAINING

Stretch, chest.

PHYSICAL TRAINING

Back

To stretch the middle of your back, start in a neutral standing position, interlock your fingers behind your head and look down. Make sure you do not arch your back at all. Your arms should add a little extra weight but make sure they do not pull on your neck.

By standing with your feet a little more than shoulder width apart and reaching over your body with your hand, you will stretch all the way down the right side of your lower back, into your hips. Stretch both sides.

To stretch your lower back, get onto your hands and knees, roll your back over and pull your belly button up into your stomach. Hold this for a few seconds then drop your stomach towards the floor. Repeat this process for thirty seconds or so.

ABOVE: Stretch, back middle.

RIGHT: Stretch, back sides.

182 PHYSICAL TRAINING

ABOVE: Stretch, back lower.

LEFT: Stretch, back lower.

Hip Flexors and Glutes

Your hip flexors are the muscles that connect your hips to your stomach. Stretching these muscles can help relieve back pain. Start with one knee on the floor and the other foot on the floor just in front of you. Push your hips forward and tuck your bum under your hips. You should feel a stretch from your leg with the knee on the floor coming up into your stomach.

To stretch your glutes, start by lying on your back and bringing your left knee up vertically to the floor. Then bring your right foot and place it sideways on your left knee. By gently pulling your left knee towards your chest you should feel a stretch across your glutes. To deepen the stretch, push your right knee away from you.

Stretch, hip flexors.

184 PHYSICAL TRAINING

ABOVE: *Stretch, glutes.*

LEFT: *Stretch, hamstrings.*

Hamstrings, Quads and Groin

Your hamstrings run from your glutes to the back of your knees. There are many ways of stretching them, depending on your flexibility level. The following is a beginners' method. Start by sitting on the floor with both legs straight out in front of you. Bend your right leg so that the sole of your foot is on the floor just in front of your hips. Now reach forward to hold onto your left foot. If you cannot reach your foot you can wrap a belt around your foot and pull on that instead.

Your quads run from the front of your hips to the front of your knees. Start standing in a neutral position then bring your right foot up to your glutes and hold it there with your hand. Keep your knees together and deepen the stretch by pushing your hips forward.

Your groin muscles run down the insides of your legs. Start by sitting down and bring both soles of your feet together next to your hips. Bring your knees down towards to floor to effect this stretch.

Stretch, quads.

186 PHYSICAL TRAINING

Stretch, groin.

Calves

This final stretch is effected by standing in front of a wall with one leg forward and one back in a small lunging position. Now place your hands against the wall and push back to feel a stretch in the calf of the back leg.

JARGON

On-sight: Climbing a route first time, without hanging on the rope or with any previous knowledge, apart from what can be seen obviously from the ground or read in the guide book.

PHYSICAL TRAINING 187

Stretch, calves.

CHAPTER 18

FINAL THOUGHT

People often repeat Alex Lowe in saying that 'the best climber in the world is the one having the most fun'. This is a great statement. It transcends grades, ethics, and styles and removes the often too prevalent competitive side of the sport.

However, I feel something is missing. Climbing is not always fun. It can be hugely frustrating, frightening, humiliating, and painful, along with exhilarating, exciting, joyous, meditative and self-affirming. These feelings have stayed with me from when I wobbled up those first few routes to my highest climbing achievements. All of these aspects of the sport are important to me. If any were missing, I would lose a piece of what makes climbing so good.

A quiet day out on some classic routes within your ability is a lot of fun. But personally, I find I miss the grand melting pot of emotions that comes from being near the edge of my current ability. The closer I am to my physical and mental limit, the more likely I am to feel a few or even all of the emotions listed above, and feel them with a clarity rarely felt in day-to-day life. For that reason I have more respect and admiration for someone screaming their way up a 6a, than watching a pro cruising up an 8a+. So I would like to adjust the quote above and leave you with one last statement.

The best climber in the world, is the one trying the hardest.

The author, trying hard but falling off on 'Welcome to the Jungle' (8a) in the Gorge de Loupe. © STEVE GORTON

INDEX

abseil (fixed)   119–193
abseil (retrievable)   123–132
abseiling   118–132
access   17
aid climbing   10

back clipping   59–60
balance   165
belay devices   23–24
belay stances (direct or indirect?)   105–106
belay stances (general rules)   92–95
belay stances (in-reach, using the rope)   96–98
belay stances (out-of-reach, using the rope)   98–101
belay stances (using a sling)   100–105
belaying (dynamic)   70–71
belaying (slamming)   68
belaying (sport climbing)   51–55
belaying (static)   69
belaying (top roping)   31–36
belaying (trad)   79–83
block leading   108–109
bolts   16
boulder pads   20–21
bouldering   8, 19

cams   75, 86–87
chalk and chalk bags   19
check each other before climbing (sport climbing)   46
check each other before climbing (top roping)   32
check each other before climbing (trad)   79
climbing shoes   19
clove hitch   94–96
communication   105–106
cow's tail   41

deep water soloing   10
double ropes   76–77, 79–81, 89
drop knee (gaining height)   168–169

escaping the system   138–144
ethics   15

fall factors   114–117
fall practice   71–72
falling   66–67

figure of eight   26–30
footwork   162–163

grades   11–13
grigri (dynamic belay)   70
grigri (lowering)   36
grigri (set up)   32–33
grigri (sport belaying)   53–55
ground anchoring (top roping)   37–39
ground anchors (sport climbing)   72

harnesses   22–23, 25
haul systems   152–155
headtorch   107
helmets   42–43
hexes   75
history   14

improvised chest harness   144–145
Italian hitch   112–113

jamming   162–164

leg behind the rope   62–63
lower-offs   55–59

magic plates   113–115
multi-pitch climbing   107–117
multi-pitching (abseiling)   125–132
multi-pitching (changeovers)   109–110
multi-pitching (rope organisation)   109–110
multi-pitching (what to carry?)   108

nut key   75
nuts   74, 83–85

passing a knot (abseiling)   155–157
passing a knot (lowering)   158–159
pitons   15
placing traditional gear   82–88
prusik knots   136–138
prusiking   151–152
prusiks (what to buy)   77

quickdraws   (sport) 40–41

190 INDEX

quickdraws (extendable) 90–92
quickdraws (in use) 47–50
quickdraws (trad) 73–74

reverso 113–115
rock over (gaining height) 166–167
rope (sport) 42
rope drag 89–90
rucksack 108

screw-gate carabiners 76
self-rescue 133–159
self-rescue (counter balance abseil) 145–148
self-rescue (rescuing and injured leader) 152
self-rescue (snatch rescue) 148–150
slings 25, 76–77
slings (as belays) 100–105
slings (placements) 88
soloing 10
sport climbing 8, 40–72
spotting 20–21
static rope 118–119
stopper knot 29–30
stretching 177–187
swinging leads 108–109

techniques 162–169
top roping 8, 22–39
traditional climbing 9, 73–106
training 160–187
training (endurance) 174
training (mental) 172
training (physical) 173–177
training (power endurance) 174
training (power) 173–174
training (technique) 170–171
training (warm down) 174–177
training (warm up) 173
tying off an Italian hitch 134–136
tying off your belay device 134–135
tying-in 26–30

water bottle 107–108
winter climbing 10
wires 74, 83–85

Yosemite lift 148, 150

Z-clipping 61–62

RELATED TITLES FROM CROWOOD

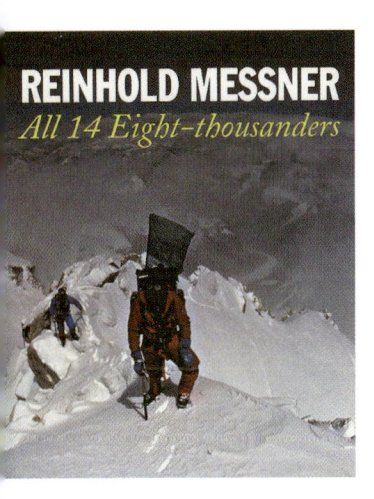

All 14 Eight-thousanders

Reinhold Messner

ISBN 978 1 86126 294 3

200 illustrations
248pp

The Crystal Horizon

Reinhold Messner

ISBN 978 1 86126 176 2

272 illustrations
324pp

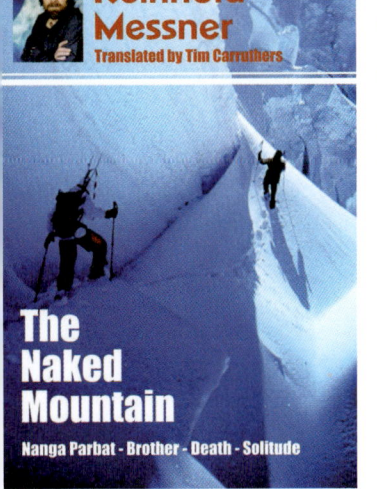

The Naked Mountain

Reinhold Messner

ISBN 978 1 86126 801 3

200 illustrations
320pp

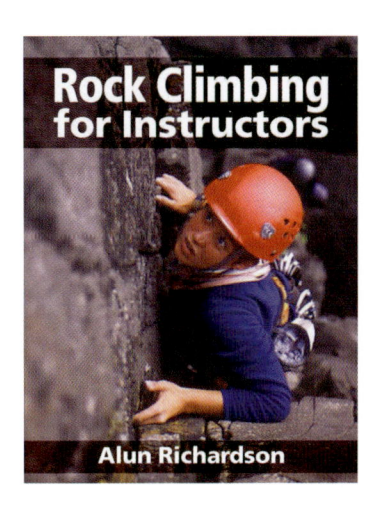

Rock Climbing for Instructors

Alun Richardson

ISBN 978 1 86126 422 0

300 illustrations
240pp

In case of difficulty in ordering, contact the Sales Office:

The Crowood Press Ltd, Ramsbury, Wiltshire SN8 2HR UK

Tel: 44 (0) 1672 520320   enquiries@crowood.com   www.crowood.com